GRAPHIC NOVELS
IN YOUR
SCHOOL LIBRARY

GRAPHIC NOVELS IN YOUR SCHOOL LIBRARY

Jesse Karp

ILLUSTRATED BY

Rush Kress

AMERICAN LIBRARY ASSOCIATION

CHICAGO   2012

For more than ten years, **JESSE KARP** has been a school librarian at LREI (Little Red School House and Elisabeth Irwin High School), one of Manhattan's oldest independent schools and a long-standing leader in progressive education. He works with students across the curriculum, from beginning readers to high school students, with all kinds of material, including graphic novels. He regularly reviews graphic novels and picture books for *Booklist* and contributes to the magazine's yearly graphic novel best list roundup; he has written articles for *Book Links* and *American Libraries* as well. He has delivered seminars on the sequential art form at Pratt Institute and Queens College and teaches a graduate course about the history and analysis of the form at Pratt. He has served as a graphic novel panelist at Book Expo America for two years running and served on YALSA's Great Graphic Novels for Teens committee from 2009 to 2012. He cocreated the education webcomic *Dr. Lollipop* and is the author of the young adult novel *Those That Wake,* which is set in Manhattan, where he lives with his wife and two daughters. Please visit his website at www.beyondwhereyoustand.com.

RUSH KRESS graduated from the illustrious Joe Kubert School of Cartoon and Graphic Illustration in 1999. He has produced corporate comics for *Derivatives Strategy* magazine, cocreated the education webcomic *Dr. Lollipop*, and produced assorted covers for *Early Music America* magazine. He lives and works in New York City.

Printed in the United States of America

16   15   14   13   12   5   4   3   2   1

Extensive effort has gone into ensuring the reliability of the information in this book; however, the publisher makes no warranty, express or implied, with respect to the material contained herein.

ISBNs: 978-0-8389-1089-4 (paper); 978-0-8389-9368-2 (PDF). For more information on digital formats, visit the ALA Store at alastore.ala.org and select eEditions.

Library of Congress Cataloging-in-Publication Data
Karp, Jesse.
    Graphic novels in your school library / Jesse Karp ; illustrated by Rush Kress.
        p.   cm.
    Includes bibliographical references and index.
    ISBN 978-0-8389-1089-4 (alk. paper)
    1. Graphic novels. 2. Graphic novels—Bibliography. 3. Libraries—Special collections—
        Graphic novels. 4. School libraries—Collection development—United States.
        5. Graphic novels in education—United States. I. Title.
    PN6710.K28 2012
    741.5—dc23   2011026353

Cover illustration by Rush Kress
Text design in Georgia and Comic Sans by Karen Sheets de Gracia and Dianne M. Rooney

♾ This paper meets the requirements of ANSI/NISO Z39.48-1992 (Permanence of Paper).

To my mother, Marilynn,
for teaching me how to use my imagination.

To my father, Ivan,
for teaching me how to express it.

And to both
for giving me the confidence to share it.

CONTENTS

PREFACE

Why This Book, Anyway?

At Reed College in Portland, Oregon, there is a most unusual library. Student-conceived at the end of the 1960s, and funded and run by students since then, it is a repository for a collection of but one thing: comic books. Standing apart from the Reed College Library, it is called the Media Lending and Loan Library (MLLL) but is better known as the Comic Book Reading Room. It was the earliest effort within the confines of an institute of education to recognize the importance of the sequential art form.

A great deal has happened to both education and the comic book since then; perhaps most surprisingly, an unlikely union between the two and a shared evolution. Many colleges and universities have recognized the production end as a valid form in which to pursue an education and a living. The Savannah College of Art and Design offers one of the top such programs in the country, but far from the only one. The Joe Kubert School of Cartoon and Graphic Art has been devoted exclusively to the study of this form since 1976.

My own experiences as a teacher and librarian bear out the worth of the medium. It will come as little surprise to anyone who works with children and young adults that graphic novels disappear from the library shelves faster than nearly anything else (except, perhaps, vampire novels, at least at the time of this writing) and are the topic of eager discussion when they find their way into classrooms. But I'm not talking just about young kids looking for some fun in a colorful narrative. I'm talking about the graduate students whom I've taught at Pratt Institute and the educators and parents at the Little Red School House and Elisabeth Irwin High School, where I work. Their fascination with the history and language of this form as a vehicle for education is clear.

Comics have long had a reputation for being disconnected from legitimate concerns; they were supposedly fluffy things, good for a laugh at best, agents of desensitization and proponents of violence at worst. These educators, librarians, and future educators and librarians are uniformly astonished and delighted to discover that the history of the comic book is the history of American culture (and not just popular culture); that the medium's evolution reflects our own cultural growing pains over the last century and defines aspects of the American psyche more trenchantly than any other art form around.

The point of all of this is merely to say that, with much credit to the invention of the term *graphic novel,* sequential art (the form of expression graphic novels are filled with) has become recognized as an art form whose history and production have something to teach us. That sequential art is a focus for education at this point can no longer be debated.

So what's the next step?

Well, the next step is already, fitfully, under way. The graphic novel is no longer just a format that it's suitable to be educated about; it is starting to see use as an actual tool with which to educate. It is not simply the production and history being recognized anymore either, but the content itself and the way it is conveyed that is becoming part of a curricular infrastructure. Already a mainstay of public libraries and having gained a foothold in school media centers, graphic novels are now finding their way into classrooms, with examples such as *Maus* and *Persepolis* drafted as supplements to history and social studies curricula. Those are two great books, to be sure, but there is so much more potential yet to be tapped.

That's what this book is for. Not the *why* of graphic novels in education, but the *how:* how to use them, when to use them, what to use them for. The key to using the format properly is to first understand it yourself. This book begins by defining the form and separating, as clearly as possible, comic books from graphic novels from manga, then provides a quick primer on the aforementioned why of graphic novels in education. From there, we break down the language and iconography of the form to get a look at its inner workings, to see what gives it such raw power. We'll then go on a quick tour of its history and see how it holds a mirror up to the world around it and, often enough, reveals what is occurring beneath the surface of that world, too.

After that, we'll get to the nitty-gritty: reading lists that will include the classics, the neoclassics, the ones everyone knows about, the ones everyone should know about, and the specialty items that it would be very good to know about. These annotated lists for every grade school age will be highlighted with notes on their specific curricular uses. Finally, I've included a number of lesson plans centered around various works or around the art form itself, for use in a variety of curricula, programs, projects, classes, and courses.

Perhaps you are a school librarian who's beginning a graphic novel collection or maintaining an established one, but you want to expand and see new ways the format can work for you and the teachers. Maybe you're a teacher who believes in the format as a worthwhile addition to the curriculum or is at least willing to give it a try, but you're not sure where to start. You are why this book was written. I have studied the medium for more than three and a half decades, first as an object of personal enthusiasm and later as a reviewer, scholar, librarian, and educator, and I've seen its incredible potential as an art form and a tool of education, a potential springing from its unique position as a nexus of two different forms of expression. The unification of these forms is able to reach parts of readers' psyches and lift their imaginations, interest, and focus to unparalleled heights.

Take advantage of this incredible potential. Use your students' enthusiasm to inspire new heights of investment in their education. That's what this book is here to help you do.

ACKNOWLEDGMENTS

I t is a rare thing to have someone who actually changed everything for you, someone who opened a new world and set you on a professional path that would define the rest of your life. I'm lucky enough to have two such people in my life.

Jennifer Hubert Swan, who took some guy off the street and forged him into a librarian. There has never been a brighter paragon of ability, professionalism, and generosity. I learn from her example and am empowered by her belief in me every day.

Stephanie Zvirin, erstwhile editor two times over, who honed my judgment and my ability to articulate it and then had the faith to offer me the opportunity of a lifetime in writing this book.

To the two of them and to the following, for their contributions to this book (and its author), I will never be able to offer adequate thanks.

Stacy Dillon, the most committed and companionable coworker a librarian could have.

Karyn Silverman, a sharper and more knowledgeable librarian is not to be found.

Larry Kaplan, for untold hours of conversation (and many more yet to come) that helped distill thoughts and opinions, and for having the audacity to suggest a teacher-run comic book club.

Phil Kassen, director of LREI, for an epic belief in the value of the school library, and for his open-mindedness to the educational possibilities of unexpected formats.

Ian Chipman, for his insight, judgment, and good humor and for keeping me in piles and piles of graphic novels on a monthly basis.

Ellen Loughran, for wisdom and know-how and, most important, the willingness to offer it to others.

All the members of ALA's Great Graphic Novels for Teens committee that I've thus far had the pleasure of working with, every one of them perceptive and discerning enough to teach even the most jaded graphic novel reader a new thing or two: Elsa Black, Emily Brown, Lisa Goldstein, Joy Kim, Candice Mack, Matthew Moffett, Barbara Moon, Kimberly Paone, Mike Pawuk, Jessica Smith, Eva Volin, Dorcas Wong, and, finally, Christian Zabriskie, whose friendship and passion have become essential to me.

And Maren, Zoe and Verity, because everything that's best in me comes from them.

PART ONE

The Form

PERHAPS YOU KNOW WHAT A GRAPHIC NOVEL IS, AT LEAST well enough to get by. How specific do you really need to get, anyway? Suppose a student comes up and says, "Isn't this just a comic book?" Or a parent demands to know what you're doing with these things in your library or classroom. Or maybe you want to know what techniques the graphic novel uses to convey its narrative and which cognitive switches are being flipped as a person reads it—the magic of the art form, as it were.

In chapter 1 I will define as completely as possible what a graphic novel is and is not (and sometimes what it both is and is not at the same time), and why it is worth using with kids and even reading yourself. In chapter 2 I'll get down to the fundamentals of how the form works, its language, codes, and symbols. This will be both a broad overview and an inquiry into the more intricate nuances so that you will be fully prepared to discuss just how and why it is a narrative art just as powerful, in its own way, as prose. Finally, in chapter 3, we'll make a brief aesthetic and philosophical comparison between American comic art and Japanese manga, which differ in some surprisingly deep and telling ways.

1

WHAT IS A GRAPHIC NOVEL AND WHY SHOULD YOU CARE?

THE FIRST THING I'M OBLIGATED TO DO IS INFORM YOU THAT graphic novels are not a genre. A genre refers to content, specifically the style or subject of the writing, such as mystery, romance, or science fiction. Because a graphic novel, just like a novel or a television program or a movie, can tell a story in any number of styles or subjects (and hence genres), a graphic novel is, like other media, a format. The graphic novel's problem in this area comes from its immediate ancestor, the comic book. The comic book has had a long-standing association with a very specific genre, namely the superhero adventure. Although the relation between comic book and graphic novel is still, in many ways, a hazy and ill-defined zone, a quick trip into a local comic store or a quick glance at a comic book rack in a local bookstore will assure you that even the comic book is no longer quite so dominated by crime fighters.

Graphic novels are a format and not a genre. Now that we have that out of the way, we can move on to more concrete definitions.

GRAPHIC NOVELS ARE NOT COMIC BOOKS . . . OR ARE THEY?

Let's be clear right off the bat that even if a graphic novel isn't a comic book, their DNA is so close as to be nearly indistinguishable. What it boils down to is sequential art, the series of illustrated panels that both formats use to tell a story. Sequential art is a related series of images ordered in a sequence so as to create a narrative. The images are generally contained within boxes called *panels.* The sequence of the panels is most often chronological (panel 1: Batman punches the Joker; panel 2: the Joker goes flying through a window), but not always. The imagery within the panels is usually figural art and, often, words appear in the panels, too. The panels themselves are mostly squares or rectangles, but not exclusively. As you can see, as with any other form of creative expression, any definition of sequential art has room for plenty of built-in exceptions. The important thing to hold onto is that sequential art is a sequence of images used to express a story or idea and that it is the form that links comic books and graphic novels inextricably together. But if that's what links them, what exactly separates them?

The term *graphic novel* was coined by comic visionary Will Eisner. Back in 1978 he wrote and illustrated *A Contract with God and Other Tenement Stories,* which was a comic book bound in paperback form with distinctly non–comic book content: Jewish life in the New York tenements of the 1920s (see fig. 1.1). Eisner wanted to elevate the form in people's minds and he wanted his work on the shelves of bookstores, where adult readers could find them, and not just on the racks of comic stores, where adult readers would surely *not* find them. So *graphic novel* is, when you get right down to it, a marketing term to make comic books seem more sophisticated or to possess a higher degree of literary merit. And it's a term that worked. Though comic books are starting to find their way into chain bookstores, graphic novels have been there for quite a while, with stores like Barnes & Noble and Borders giving them their own sizable sections. This is also how comic book publishers employ the term these days: to differentiate their comic books, which tend to appeal to specialty audiences, from their graphic novels, which attract a wider market. It will be very helpful to remember that the term *graphic novel* is little more than a business decision. That's okay, though; many of the decisions that have evolved sequential art over the years were inspired by profit-inducing strategies conceived of by men in suits around conference room tables. But make sure to hear what the men in suits are *not* telling you: most graphic novels are really comic books after all—that is, containing not original material, but collected material from monthly comic books.

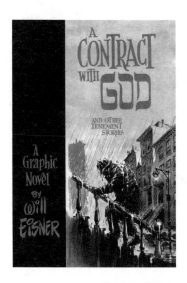

Most graphic novels produced in this country are published by the two biggest comic book companies: Marvel Comics and DC Comics. But these graphic novels are, for the most part, reprinted collections of comics that have already been serialized on a monthly schedule. Most graphic novels containing original material are produced by the independent comic market or by established publishing houses such as Simon and Schuster, Random House, and First Second. Based on statistics from the Graphic Novel Archive website, of the 12,294 graphic novels that had been cataloged as of 2010, 5,939 (48.31%) of them are collections of previously published material (i.e., mostly superhero graphic novels). A mere 424 (3.45%) contain original, stand-alone material (e.g., *Persepolis* or *Fun Home*). Another 5,645 (45.92%) are defined as serialized graphic novels, most of which are manga collected and translated from the original Japanese material. (Statistics provided by the very helpful webmaster extraordinaire Jeff Bogumil at the Graphic Novel Archive, http://graphicnovelarchive.com.) Clearly, the vast majority of what is considered a graphic novel is collected material.

So, are we to distinguish between collections and original works? I'm afraid it's too late for that, since they've all been referred to under the blanket term *graphic novel* since practically their inception. Publishers surely don't want us to make that distinction because it could rob the collections of the extra gravitas and respectability that the term affords them. And we don't really want to, anyway, because it would make cataloging them a nightmare (more of a nightmare, I should say) and such a distinction would likely prove confusing for our patrons, students, and readers. So the term *graphic novel* encompasses books containing sequential art that is either original or collected.

Unfortunately, this still leaves us with the question of whether comics and graphic novels are any different and, if so, how. On the way to a final answer, let's examine some of the common notions on the subject.

Here's a popular one: graphic novels contain more sophisticated, mature, and "worthwhile" content than comic books. Given the facts about reprinted stories, it should be patently clear that this isn't true. If a majority of graphic novels actually contain material from comic books, they can't very well be thematically different in their approach or content from the comics they collect, can they?

Have a look at another generally accepted criterion for distinguishing comics from graphic novels: graphic novels tell a full story from beginning to end, even if it's over the course of several volumes, while comic books have an open-ended continuity that could run on indefinitely. Again, the issue of collections makes this hard to accept. If many graphic novels simply collect a series of comics that are running a potentially infinite story, how could the graphic novels not have that same potential, regardless of whether more of that story is told between two covers? However, there is some truth to the idea that even graphic novels that are collections tend to give a sense of closure to their stories within a single volume. A standard collection of the latest Spider-Man comics (for instance) will tell an arc of story that completes a specific adventure of the character but leaves several overarching themes and elements developing for further issues and collections.

This is, as it happens, an intentional practice on the part of comic book publishers these days. Monthly comic books are written in these six- or seven-issue arcs specifically so that they can be collected and marketed in this way. As I mentioned, the real money is in getting graphic novels to bookstore shoppers and not just to comic store shoppers. In order to appeal to the bookstore crowd, you want to give them the sense that they're getting a full story for their money but also leave it opened enough that if they enjoyed it, they'll come back for the next volume. This is a practice that went into full swing at about the time Marvel Comics really dived into graphic novel publishing (the company was years behind competitor DC in a strong program for collecting its work in graphic novel form). More specifically still, the consistent story and standard can be traced to Marvel's launch of its Ultimate imprint with *Ultimate Spider-Man* (see fig. 1.2). *Ultimate Spider-Man* was a retelling of Spider-Man's origin and subsequent adventures in an updated setting (rather than in the early 1960s, when the character was actually created). Writer Brian Michael Bendis spearheaded a style of comic book writing that told stories within these easily collectible dramatic arcs. The first seven issues of *Ultimate Spider-Man* not only told the story of Peter Parker's transformation into a superhero, but also contained the origin of and showdown with his archenemy, the Green Goblin. By comparison, the original version of this tale in the *Amazing Spider-Man* title published in the 1960s—encompassing just the introduction of the Green Goblin, the revelation of his secret identity, and the dramatic (but not actually final) showdown between the opponents—ran from issue numbers 14 through 40. That's twenty-six issues, featuring a number of other character introductions and narrative elements that had nothing to do with the Green Goblin, published over the course of a little more than two years and, obviously, not written with the intention of collecting them for the bookstore market.

So individual graphic novels tell full stories (or arcs), while individual comics don't. This is, unfortunately for clarity's sake, not a hard-and-fast rule, but it does tend to apply. As should be obvious from the Spider-Man example above, as older comic books are collected into graphic novel form, it's impossible to adhere to this rule consistently.

What, then, is the absolute, incontrovertible distinction between graphic novel and comic book? Well . . . there isn't one. Sorry. But we can get considerably more clear-cut on the issue by looking at matters of physical form.

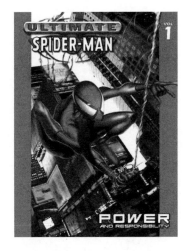

FIGURE 1.2

Ultimate Spider-Man Volume 1: Power and Responsibility. Spider-Man and all other Marvel characters: TM and © 2002 Marvel Entertainment, LLC, and its subsidiaries. All rights reserved.

Put simply, comic books are floppy and graphic novel are not. Comics are bound with staples and usually run twenty-two pages (though they can run up to one hundred). Graphic novels are bound like novels, hardcover or paperback, and usually run upward of sixty-four pages (though they do sometimes run down to forty-eight pages). Both formats have a range of physical dimensions (though more so with graphic novels) and so we're really better off not bothering with those. There is, to confuse things further, a comic book format known as *prestige,* most popular back in the 1980s and early 1990s. These comics were bound as trade paperbacks and ran forty-eight pages or higher. They were, in many ways, the precursor of the modern graphic novel and are seldom produced any more. It would be fair to say, in sum, that as physical objects comic books and graphic novels can be different, but as an art form they are the same. So, by and large, you are safe identifying a graphic novel with this rock solid, nonabstract, definition of physical form, eschewing the content for means of definition. It is not, as we are about to see, the last time we will need to eschew content to clear the table and make a final statement about what a graphic novel is.

Graphic Novels Are Not Novels
. . . or Are They?

You will notice that the term *graphic novel* is used even when the material in question is a biography (say, *Persephone* by Marjane Satrapi), current events analysis (say, *The 9/11 Report* by Jacobson and Colon), or a historical record (say, *Gettysburg: The Graphic Novel* by Butzer). This has frustrated many because it appears to be inaccurate. A novel is a story, a work of fiction, whereas things such as biographies, current event analyses, and historical records are clearly not fiction. There's been a call from some quadrants to rename the format. Some suggestions I've heard are *graphic format,* which sounds a bit stiff and technical; *graphic book,* which suggests that the content features extreme violence or sexuality; *graphic narrative,* which does not seem to specifically refer to a physical object; *graphics,* which is easily confused with the same term used for images and illustrations; and *sequential art book,* which is a bit unwieldy and probably somewhat on the confusing side for people who haven't heard the term *sequential art* before. A written abbreviation often used, and one I'll be using myself in later chapters, is *GN,* which allows us to both keep the term intact and hide it at the same time.

It's a moot point, in any event. The issue is by and large ignored by the general readership, which would no doubt be confused by a rejiggering now that the format has been so well established and gained such respect under its current name. Whether or not it would even be possible to change the term now that it has been accepted into the cultural lexicon is beside the point.

Let's return to where we started the chapter, with the conceptual. Just as graphic novel is a format (having to do with physical form) and not a genre (having to do with content), the word *novel* should be taken as a reference not to the content of the work, but rather to its physical form. It is, essentially, sequential art with the physical form most reminiscent of a novel, which is to say, bound as a hardcover or softcover book, rather than a comic. If we can accept the idea that the term as well as the object itself is defined by its physical form rather than by its content, then we can all relax and get on with important stuff.

Here it is, then, all in one neat sentence: a graphic novel is a generally complete narrative told in sequential art, bound on sturdy paper without staples.

WHY YOU SHOULD CARE

As I said in the introduction, this book is about *how* graphic novels can tie into education, not why they *should*. Nevertheless, I recognize that this isn't a done deal for much of the ed-ucation world. For the record, and as quickly as possible, let's get the *why* out of the way.

In their seminal *Graphic Novels in Your Media Center,* Allyson and Barry Lyga identify three types of burgeoning readers to whom the format proves a particular benefit:

"Slow visualizers," who have trouble creating mental images from word descriptions (a skill essential to reading) and can be intimidated by long passages of text, benefit from the graphic novel's "visual cueing systems that not only balance the text but also help the student interpret it" (Lyga and Lyga 2004).

"Reluctant readers," who lack motivation to pick up or enjoy books, "don't consider graphic novels to be 'real' books [and so do] not mind reading them" (Lyga and Lyga 2004).

"Visually dependent" students, victims of the all-encompassing visual media that inundates children every day, tend to eschew books because books are too slow moving or have no visual component to keep interest engaged (Lyga and Lyga 2004). Graphic novels, naturally, tend to stimulate interest in these students much faster than books.

In every case, graphic novels build skills, confidence, and desire to move on to other formats and to continue reading just for the sake of enjoyment. There is, of course, an obligation to teach these students to go deeper than the surface image, and graphic novels nurture a form of visual literacy that "goes beyond the presented graphics and looks at the messages, meanings, and motivation behind a visual image" (Lyga and Lyga 2004).

According to Drego Little in "In a Single Bound: A Short Primer on Comics for Educators," the form "appears simple at first but is actually a complex cognitive task" (Little 2005). Three primary phenomena occur, interconnected and overlapping, when reading sequential art. They are:

closure—the brain's capacity to create complete images out of partial ones, to fill in gaps and construct a sequence where none specifically exists

narrative density—the interpretation of the full range of many layers of information that a single panel can convey

amplification—the ability of pictures and words to scaffold one another to support full comprehension (Little 2005)

"Because the images and the words are both working to convey the same story arc, comics provide a type of literacy support no other medium does" (Little 2005). Children who read comics growing up even show a larger vocabulary and a better understanding of verb tenses than children who do not (Smetana 2009). Indeed, countries with high national literacy rates also tend to have a thriving comic culture, one that is respected by adult interest and has authority figure approval, such as Finland and Japan (Little 2005).

With information like this to build on, sequential art gains ever more purchase as a pedagogical tool. In New York, Columbia University's Teachers College has created the Comic Book Project, a program that uses sequential art creation to expand children's interest in reading and story creation. Since the program began in an elementary school in Queens, New York, "it has expanded to 860 schools across the country" as teachers realize that "for kids who may be struggling and for kids who may be new to the English language, that visual sequence is a very powerful tool" (Gootman 2007).

Indeed, in the spring of 2008 the New York Department of Education began a program to train many of the city's school librarians in selecting and teaching graphic novels as a tool to inspire student's interest in reading and literacy.

Yet another application was found in a state school in Northern California engaged in a literacy program for deaf students in 2008. Given that a deaf person's primary means of communication is visual, it seemed a natural fit. Sure enough, the teachers found great success in both building interest in their deaf students and raising comprehension levels because "due to their visual nature, comics and graphic novels provide a context-rich, high-interest story environment for acquiring new vocabulary" (Smetana 2009).

In the face of all this, you may still hear the cry go up that graphic novels are merely "picture books for older kids" and that the visual element simply makes it a reading shortcut and lowers comprehension. A study conducted by Mallia Gorg, however, counters this handily. Gorg represented the same story in three different forms: one as written text, another as written text with a small number of illustrations, and a last version in classic comic book style with sequential panels of art and words. Three different groups of students were presented with one version each and then asked questions to determine comprehension level. The results showed no significant difference whatsoever in the test scores, proving that the comic version was just as effective as the more traditional two in putting across the story and message (Gorg 2007).

The heart of the matter is, perhaps, best summed up by James Sturm, a graphic novel writer and artist and director of Vermont's Center for Cartoon Studies, who noted that "there is plenty of information out there. Google and Wikipedia can provide a biography in seconds. It is stories that give information meaning. Compelling stories make readers want to learn or do more" (Karp 2008).

Graphic novels, in other words, help students invest in their own education.

2

HOW DO GRAPHIC NOVELS WORK?

SEQUENTIAL ART COMBINES WORDS, WHICH APPEAL TO THE intellect, and pictures, which appeal to the emotions, in a way that no other art form does. Unlike picture books, the words and pictures in sequential art coexist in the same conceptual space (the panel) and are joined into a single piece (usually via word balloons). Unlike movies, the words and pictures in sequential art are perceived at the speed the reader desires and with the same sense (visually), and thus have a unique and essential unity in the way the reader experiences them. By joining the intellect and the emotions together as it does, sequential art has a vast and unique potential for creating powerful narrative.

However, to tell a story in sequential art, something vital is required: a sequence. Without the images relating to one another, you may have some interesting things to look at, but you don't have a story any more than you would if you joined unrelated words together. And, like words, the images must relate in a specifically chronological and contextual way. One image must lead into the next and the next, thus creating a sequence. And for a sequence to exist, time must pass, because that's what a sequence is: related incidents occurring one after the other. For "after" to occur, time must pass. That's really the secret of this entire enterprise called sequential art. It is, at its very core, a manner of showing you that time is passing. Even within a single panel, it is often necessary to arrange images in a sequence for this purpose. That's the sequential. The art, of course, is in *how* you make the time appear to pass. It is within this span that expression comes to bear, revealing action, emotion, character, and everything else necessary to a compelling story.

Sequential art has only three tools at its disposal for creating this illusion. These are (1) the gutter (the space in between panels), (2) symbols and codes, and (3) words. Essentially, everything you see in a comic or GN will adhere to one or more of these three techniques, which we will now explore individually and at length.

GETTING YOUR MIND INTO THE GUTTER

Time cannot actually pass within a still image, and if that time cannot pass *within* the panels, then there's only one place left for time to do its business: *in between* the panels. The space in between two panels, be it a vast channel or a nearly invisible millimeter of dark line, is known as the *gutter*. An artist strives to create the perception of passing time by using this internecine space; to, in effect, make *us* create the passage of time within the gutter merely by suggesting that passage in the panels on either side of it.

What's happening, exactly, in figure 2.1? The man jumped, right? Wrong, actually. The first panel within figure 2.1 shows the man about to jump, and the second panel shows him landing. No actual jump has occurred in that sequence, except for the jump you created by following the artist's suggestions. The two panels in figure 2.1 depict a man jumping without actually showing a jump. The gutter is where a skilled artist will make you do all the work. Depending on the skill of the artist, or the effect he is trying to achieve, he can let more or less action or time occur within the gutter.

FIGURE 2.1

What have we got in figure 2.2? There's a man actually jumping, right? Wrong again. A man can't actually jump in still images, no matter how many there are. Figure 2.2 is in fact the same as figure 2.1 with the addition of a middle panel in which a man is frozen in the air. The depiction of the jump here is rather more explicit, and playing with this simple sequence can reveal the artist's motives and perhaps even the nature of the story he's trying to tell. The simpler sequence in figure 2.1 suggests the same jump, but it's a quicker way of showing the action. This leaves room in other places for what the artist deems more important story elements.

Heading further away from the simplicity of figure 2.1, you have figure 2.3. Here, again, is the same jump, but with rather more specific moments depicted. You see not only the jump, but perhaps how difficult the jump is, how agile the man jumping is, how far the two cliff edges are. This takes up more space and conveys more drama and suggests that this story may be more action oriented. Superhero comics commonly feature a high panel-to-action ratio, lavishing space on fisticuffs and giving rather less space to straightforward dialogue, for instance. Little surprise, since superhero stories are, in many ways, about action, and the characters themselves are defined not only by the actions they take, but also by the

FIGURE 2.2

specific ways they take them. You don't imagine Spider-Man engaging in the same kind of fight that Superman does, right? Spider-Man bounces off walls, dodges bullets, spins webs from a distance, leaps in for quick punches and kicks. Superman is an unstoppable force, implacable, warding off bullets by merely standing still and throwing large punches to devastating effect. That says something about the characters, and to define those things, their actions need to be quite detailed. There are other comics, meanwhile, that fill entire pages with dozens of panels of two heads talking. Granted, this is a more experimental, indie-spirited kind of a page composition, but just flipping through the two different styles will quickly tell you how time is intended to pass and thus what sort of a story to expect.

FIGURE 2.3

The panel itself, the actual borders that define the space of the image, are malleable, too. Generally speaking, simple and uncrowded page composition transmits a story most effectively, but there are exceptions. Splash pages (full-page images) are fairly common in action-oriented comics to give an even greater scale or impact. Occasionally a panel effect can be used to transmit subtle nuances. Because the panel borders determine our perception of the space the story exists in, a panel shape like the one in figure 2.4 can alter our sense of distance or time as, here, we have a more thoughtful and majestic tone than the previous "action shots."

FIGURE 2.4

The story is not just *in* the panels, but just as important, *in between* the panels, not to mention what the very lines of the panels themselves have to say.

But, since I mentioned it, what exactly is in the panels, anyway?

#&@$$&

Within a single panel of sequential art, there's plenty to see. Even disregarding the figural images, there's often an array of things to interpret. There are words, of course, but before we even get to those, there's a form of language even more rudimentary. If time is to be made to pass within a single panel, if there is any action to be taken, then it is this language that will drive the image, suggest animation to us much as the gutter does in between the panels. These are symbols and codes that function as the specific language of sequential art and have become so integrated into the experience that we generally take them for granted. We take in only the effect of these symbols, just as we don't spend time interpreting a question mark at the end of a sentence.

The most common symbol in sequential art is the word balloon, the white bubble that indicates its speaker with a pointed stem. The balloons are meant to hold words, but still ignoring those words, the balloons themselves can have a variety of meanings. Figure 2.5 contains four sorts of word balloons: (1) a speech balloon, (2) a whisper balloon, (3) a thought balloon, and (4) a shouting balloon. These symbols function such that you don't even need to look inside the balloon to get a sense of what is being expressed.

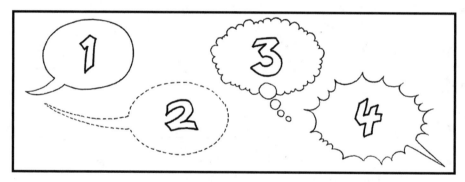

FIGURE 2.5

As I said, the balloons generally contain words. However, other symbols can sometimes express an idea just as elegantly. Put a lone question mark within a speech or thought balloon and you understand what the character is feeling. Put a "&$#@!" inside a shout balloon and . . . you see where I'm going.

Leaving the word balloons behind, there's still an awful lot with which to work. The most elementary way to convey the passage of time in sequential art is through movement, and if you need to do that in a single panel you've got a few choices. Remember our jumper? Figure 2.6 matches the middle panel from figure 2.2, but this time it has speed lines indicating his progress. The same fellow is making the same jump, but the motion, or speed, lines convey his movement within the single panel, dramatizing the effect of the jump without extraneous panels.

In figure 2.7 we have the same jumper again, this time with the ghosting or doubling effect behind him, showing a detailed progress of his entire jump. This has the effect of hyperfocusing the reader on the action, highlighting it much as slow motion would in film.

FIGURE 2.6

FIGURE 2.7

Going beyond motion, there is a vast array of symbols constructed to give a sense of emotion and conditions. The first panel in figure 2.8 depicts a plate of food. Would you care for a bite of this food? Perhaps you should wait a bit because it's quite hot, as indicated by the heat symbols rising from it. In the second panel, a man hoping for a plate of ice cream or perhaps some cool lemonade after a hot day's work instead finds hot food waiting. How does he feel about it? I'm sure you can tell, even though you can't see his face or hear his words, as the anger lines emanating from him make it plain.

These examples barely scratch the surface of the vast lexicon of symbols and codes used in sequential art. If you think about it, I'm sure you can conjure a few, even if you've barely cracked a comic book in your life. The argument can be made, of course, that sequential art functions solely on symbols. What is an image after all, but a form of symbol? The more obscure the representation is from the actual thing being represented, the more acute our interpretive abilities must be. Take a face, for example. The less specific an image becomes,

FIGURE 2.8

FIGURE 2.9

the more symbolic it appears. The face in figure 2.9 is the most abstract (that is, most obscure from the actual object) way you can possibly reproduce the thing known as a face in symbols and still recognize it, right? As Scott McCloud pointed out in his seminal (and incomparable) *Understanding Comics,* you can, in fact, depict a face still more abstractly. Here's how: FACE (Harper 1994). Letters and words are the most common form of iconography we have, and their symbiosis with images is the power of sequential art.

IF A PICTURE IS WORTH A THOUSAND WORDS, HOW MANY WORDS IS A PICTURE WITH WORDS IN IT WORTH?

First and foremost, the very presence of spoken words within a panel demands the passage of time. How can a word be spoken unless time is passing? In figure 2.10, the first panel shows us, merely through its use of spoken word, a moment of time passing. The second shows us a longer stretch of time passing, all within a single panel.

FIGURE 2.10

    Let's look at the way the words themselves are portrayed. What is being said or thought certainly tells us something about a character, but so does the manner in which it's being said or thought. In figure 2.11, the first panel conveys the thought and feeling. The second panel makes the point somewhat more forcefully—not just in the shape of the word balloon, but also in the font of the letters themselves. Still more dramatic is the sense of isolation, sorrow, and uncertainty conveyed in the third panel, specifically because of the size and lightness of the words within the balloon.

    Outside the confines of a single panel, words change and sometimes even create the relationship between images, the very sequence itself. In figure 2.12, the first sequence certainly tells you what's happening, but the second sequence gives a stronger sense of continuity between the panels and heightens the tension of the moment.

FIGURE 2.11

 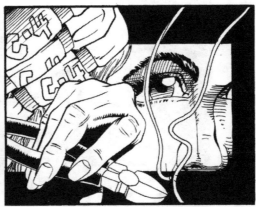

FIGURE 2.12

Subtle shadings are created by making choices about word placement, such as in figures 2.13 and 2.14. The first panel does not particularly cry out for attention to the emotional undercurrents of the situation. The sequence of panels beneath suggests a more noteworthy message.

And that's just the spoken word.

The caption, the free-floating box in the panel that contains narration, has fallen into far less use in sequential art these days. Back in the golden age of the panel, they were as integral to the sequential art experience as the word balloons themselves, panels often crowded with both description and conversation (the old EC Comics of the 1950s are a prime example of this style). As the sophistication of the art has grown, however, storytellers have found that

FIGURE 2.13

FIGURE 2.14

narration, especially that which duplicates the message given by the image within the same panel, tends to bog down the story. These days, images and dialogue function elegantly on their own, in most instances. There are, however, some cases in which the caption remains integral.

The subjective narration of a character depicted within a caption can give a cinematic voice-over quality to a story at the same time that it illuminates character and motive. The image in figure 2.15 is surely made more intense by the narration, more so than it would have been in a thought balloon, as the caption gives a greater sense of removal, disassociation, and omniscience.

FIGURE 2.15

The caption is also still the most effective way of tying images into a sequence when there might otherwise appear to be no connection whatsoever. The first sequence in figure 2.16 may as well not even be a sequence for all the connection it has. But add a single word to the second panel and you have an instant contextual connection, thus illustrating the difference between what is merely art in sequence and what is sequential art.

FIGURE 2.16

The gutter, symbols and codes, and words are the three methods that sequential art uses to convey the passage of time and to highlight the storytelling necessities of character and emotion. I'm going to go ahead and say that you will not find a piece of narrative sequential art that doesn't conform to this rule (and, yes, I have come across rare exceptions). But within these three methods is a vast array of possibility, and every culture, to say nothing of every artist, puts its own stamp on the art form.

3

DISREPUTABLE PICTURES
A Brief Word about Manga

WHILE THIS IS BY NO MEANS A BOOK ABOUT MANGA, ANY discussion of sequential art at this point in time must involve some consideration of the Japanese form, given its astonishing rise in popularity since 2000. *Manga* (pronounced mahn-ga, *not* mayn-ga) is a Japanese word meaning "disreputable pictures" or "whimsical pictures" and, to be succinct about it, is simply the Japanese version of a comic book. Ah, but even within that straightforward distinction there is room for a great deal of divergence.

Comics have had a long hard climb for widespread respectability in the United States (which they're still struggling through in many ways). Other cultures have long been more accepting of the form, to some extent because no other culture has seen the form dominated by a single genre like we have (that would be superheroes, a genre mainly associated with children's interests). France, in particular, has an extensive history of more adult-oriented fare within the medium, referring to the form as "the Ninth Art." However, no place has it over Japan in this regard. In an astonishing figure, 22 percent of all printed material in Japan is manga. This is no doubt the result of the fact that manga covers a vast range of genres and is aimed at so many different interests and reading levels. There is no shame in cracking one open, regardless of age. Riding the subway in Tokyo, you are likely to see "graying salarymen, twenty-something [sic] hipsters, and schoolgirls all paging through a manga" (Pink 2007).

Even in the United States, the power of manga has become undeniable. Between 2003 and 2007, manga sales in the United States tripled (Pink 2007), and between 2000 and 2006, manga went from "a third of the $75 million graphic novel industry to claiming almost two-thirds of what is now a $330 million movement" (Thompson 2007). Even given the vast $255 million rise in the income over six years of the GN industry itself, when it comes to manga "nothing in the bookstore market has seen that sort of evolution in such a short time" (Thompson 2007).

What, exactly, makes manga so popular with our kids? So many of the animated television programs and video games that children and young adults are consuming are created and produced in Japan; everything from Pokemon to the ever-popular Naruto series. The aesthetic sensibility of the manga, in particular, has become a permanent fixture of the American cultural landscape and a visual language with which kids and young adults feel comfortably familiar. As the manga style of art and storytelling becomes so popular, it's little wonder that American artists and publishers are beginning to adapt and synthesize it into the production of American comics.

So just what are some of these differences, anyway?

DEATHMATCH: MANGA VERSUS COMICS

Let's get this obvious one out of the way first. Manga in its original Japanese form is meant to be read from right to left, and is thus designed that way. This isn't just a matter of the page and panel sequence, but applies to the imagery and word balloons within the panels themselves. Many manga are reproduced in this country with the original sequence intact, and reading them can take some getting used to. While this is a significant difference in form, it does not change the inherent nature of the stories. Indeed, there are plenty of manga reproduced for this country that reverse the original sequence into a familiar left-to-right order, and this has no essential effect on the content.

Comic book and GN content fall into various genres. Superheroes still tend to rule the form around here, but crime and horror are gaining ground and there's humor, sci-fi, and adult popping around, too, and at least a few examples of pretty much any genre interest you could think of. However, manga focuses genre through the lens of gender and age in a very specific way, targeting not only reading levels and genre interest, but also gender in a clear, intentional manner that American publishers do not. *Shonen* is boys' manga: action, sci-fi, fantasy, and sports (nearly an unheard of subject in American comics). *Shojo* is girls' manga and focuses on romance, mystery, and horror. *Seinen* and *josei* are manga targeted at older men and women, respectively (generally college age and up) and reflect this not only in genre choice, but also in maturity and extremity of content. Manga has embraced the divergent demographics of its readership and so has ended up with a wider and more immediate appeal to female readership and to older, more serious adult readers, audiences that GNs are just now beginning to lure at significant rates. One area in which manga flags by comparison is—can you guess?—the superhero genre. Why did the American comic form embrace superheroes so wholeheartedly? The answer is pent up in the history of the form and will be addressed in the next chapter.

What about the stories themselves? On a series-to-series basis, comics are generally open-ended; their stories and characters tend to run on and on until and if a dwindling readership makes it financially inadvisable to continue. Manga series are usually finite, running anywhere from four to thirty volumes, though not as a rule. The point is that a manga series is conceived as a story with a beginning, a middle, and an end, while comics generally are not.

Those are some all-encompassing ways in which the formats themselves differ. But what about content? The first thing you come to when you open either one is the art, and the first thing you'll notice is that comics are nearly always in color, while manga are, by vast majority, not. But that's merely the surface.

Although we're starting to see aspects of the manga aesthetic in American comics, there is little mistaking the art style in one for the other. Depending on the genre, manga figural art tends to contain more extreme stylization than comics, the figures being more pliable, elongated, and what many would call "cartoonish," as seen in figure 3.1. The art is, by and large, less literal, if you will, often intended to suggest the emotion of the character or situation rather than the actual appearance.

FIGURE 3.1

Itazura Na Kiss, © Kaoru Tada/ minato-pro-Mz-Plan. All rights reserved. Original Japanese edition published in 2008 by FAIRBELL Corporation, Tokyo. English translation rights arranged with FAIRBELL Corporation, Tokyo. English translation © 2009 Digital Manga, Inc.

Meanwhile, manga background or object art tends toward realism of an intensely acute variety. Images of guns (as in figure 3.2), cars, trees, buildings, can be so realistic that they border on the fetishistic.

Deeper philosophical differences emerge. Take this action sequence from a comic in figure 3.3 and compare it to the action sequence from a manga in figure 3.4. The panels in the Spider-Man comic depict the pose of a strike, the look on a face at impact. The only sound effects here are the sounds of that impact, and each such impact is highlighted by

FIGURE 3.2

Hellsing Volume 1 (1998). HELLSING volume 1 © KOHTA HIRANO 1998. Originally published in Japan in 1998 by SHONEN GAHOSHA Co., Ltd., TOKYO. English translation rights arranged with SHONEN GAHOSHA Co., Ltd., TOKYO through TOHAN CORPORATION, TOKYO. English translation copyright Dark Horse Comics, Inc./Digital Manga, Inc.

FIGURE 3.3

Ultimate Spider-Man #7. Spider-Man and all other Marvel characters: TM and © 2010 Marvel Entertainment, LLC. and its subsidiaries. All rights reserved.

FIGURE 3.4

Hellsing Volume 1 (1998). HELLSING volume 1 © KOHTA HIRANO 1998. Originally published in Japan in 1998 by SHONEN GAHOSHA Co., Ltd., TOKYO. English translation rights arranged with SHONEN GAHOSHA Co., Ltd., TOKYO through TOHAN CORPORATION, TOKYO. English translation copyright Dark Horse Comics, Inc./Digital Manga, Inc.

a "flash of light" effect. Even the motion effects, as when Spider-Man is being thrown by his enemy, make it look as though he's blasting away like a rocket ship. The panels in the manga *Hellsing,* though they certainly contain impact, are about the effort of the movement leading up to it, the motion of the characters, as highlighted both by the riot of speed lines that make figures seem a blur of motion and the sound effects that spring from the effort behind the movements and the sound of air being cut by motion. From these representative examples we can gather something crucial about the nature of the individual media. American sequential art is about action, which is to say the *effect* of movement. Manga strives to capture the action as it happens, which is to say the *movement itself.* Does the American interest in result and the Japanese concentration on process say something salient about the cultures themselves? You will have to be the judge of that.

As we look at the art as a visual language—as we discussed at length in the last chapter— some more extreme differences become evident. This should come as no surprise because symbols and visual codes develop from a culture's deeper understanding of itself. The more distinct the cultures, the more distinct their symbols. Another whole book could be filled with an analysis of manga's own codes and symbols. For the sake of a simple example, let's look at one that points up the more obvious differences between manga and American comics.

Where we tend to let a character's facial expressions, or the situation they're in, spell out their emotional condition, manga will often add a descriptive effect. These can be utterly literal, as in figure 3.5.

FIGURE 3.5

Itazura Na Kiss. © Kaoru Tada/minato-pro-Mz-Plan. All rights reserved. Original Japanese edition published in 2008 by FAIRBELL Corporation, Tokyo. English translation rights arranged with FAIRBELL Corporation, Tokyo. English translation © 2009 Digital Manga, Inc.

They can also be more whimsical, as with the *chibi* version of the face in the second panel of figure 3.6, who is the same character as the more realistic one in the first panel of the same figure. *Chibi* (meaning "short person" or "small child") are small or cartoonishly extreme versions of a character in the midst of emotional moments or difficult decisions, whose facial expressions or speech reflect the emotional issue at stake.

FIGURE 3.6

Hellsing Volume 1 (1998). HELLSING volume 1 © KOHTA HIRANO 1998. Originally published in Japan in 1998 by SHONEN GAHOSHA Co., Ltd., TOKYO. English translation rights arranged with SHONEN GAHOSHA Co., Ltd., TOKYO through TOHAN CORPORATION, TOKYO. English translation copyright Dark Horse Comics, Inc./Digital Manga, Inc.

These are simply two of the codes that manga uses to make the emotional lives of its characters more evident with conceptual techniques, an abstraction playing in the "real world" of the story. This prevalence of abstract or spiritual elements in manga, which are largely absent from comics and GN, again speak to the very nature of the cultures that produce these forms.

American comics favor a cause-and-effect philosophy, a result-oriented style, and they are more literal, more concrete and material oriented in their depictions. As manga favors not the result as much as the path to it, the value of a flowing process, it is also more comfortable with depictions of the abstract or spiritual elements that seem to have little place in comics. These are not hard-and-fast rules that apply to every example within each medium. This area has received little study and so at this time remains largely theoretical. (To my knowledge there has been no work whatsoever examining these deeper thematic concerns in comparison, leaving a crucial area of cultural comparison wide open to the right scholar.)

Manga is a format that is absolutely worth your time to examine more closely elsewhere, as its popularity among young readers demands. Although I will touch on examples of it as we go, it is not our focus here. Sequential art was born in the United States and in many ways is still a uniquely American form. As we're about to see, its history and evolution reveal significant messages about our own society and culture.

PART TWO

A History of American Sequential Art

THE PUBLIC INITIALLY PERCEIVED COMICS AS A SILLY LITTLE distraction lacking any relation to serious concerns—a fantasy window into a frivolous world of goofy animals and costumed musclemen. This same public was quick to form a collective lynch mob when they saw that comics, in fact, had too much to say about the world, and the medium was marched before a Senate subcommittee to meet its fate. From one extreme to another, the intricate intertwined evolution of comics and the culture they exist in has generally been overlooked. It will come as a shock to many that the costumed muscleman, the very one who defined the course of comics forever but is still so easily scowled at, was born of a potent chemistry of social current and psychological nuance. In part II I'm going to trace the evolution of the medium, from the seeds it grew out of to the (more or less) well-respected art form it became. My intention here is not to flood you with names and dates, but to familiarize you with the developing personality of the form, and just how much it has been informed by and how much it has to say about the cultural, social, political, and economic realities of the world we inhabit.

In chapter 4 we'll look at the form's beginnings, how strips grew into books, and how certain creators set up the powerful elements that would eventually pave the way for the GN. In chapter 5 we'll examine those elements more specifically and trace the rise of the GN to its present state.

My hope is that this will not only enhance your understanding of GNs, but will also allow you to cull greater nuance from the stories within, nuances you can explore with your students.

4

THE COMIC BOOK

THE COMIC BOOK (AND THE ART FORM FROM WHICH IT'S CON-
stituted) is one of only two uniquely American art forms (jazz being the other). Although
other countries have a proud comic history in their own right (particularly France and
Japan, as previously discussed), the comic book was born here; it was our culture that gave
it shape, our psyches that imbued it with the electric charge of life. In this chapter we will
explore how images combined with words and grew into a widespread form that by turns
delighted and infuriated America and how the comic book itself became a mainstay of the
American cultural landscape.

THE PREHISTORY

It may be tempting to look at Egyptian hieroglyphics, or even cave paintings, to find the
seeds of sequential art. However, neither really offered narratives per se. They were individual images (cave paintings) or they were not pictorial representations of actual objects
and people, but representations of sounds, used to reproduce words just as our alphabet
does (hieroglyphics). They both do illustrate, though, how integral imagery is to human
expression.

Egyptian painting holds stronger ties, being the earliest examples of stories told in
a sequence of images. From there, we have numerous examples throughout history that
resemble the sequential art form: stained-glass window sequences, illuminated manu-
scripts, and the medieval European Bayeux Tapestry; and with the invention of printing,

FIGURE 4.1

Frans Masereel woodcut sequence. © Artists Rights Society (ARS), New York/VG Bild-Kunst, Bonn

the array of such illustrated matter becomes vast. William Hogarth's 1731 "A Harlot's Progress" is undeniably a story told in a sequence of related images. More recent, and perhaps most significant to the specific evolution of sequential art, were the early twentieth-century woodcut narratives of artists such as Lynd Ward and Frans Masereel, as seen in figure 4.1.

However, sequential art as it exists in modern comics and GNs is distinguished by its own language, formula, and nuances that do not appear in any of the above. The path of telling a story in a sequence of images may have diffuse origins, but the true language of sequential art began in a comfortably precise spot.

THE FUNNIES

The first political cartoons appeared as early as 1754, in Ben Franklin's *Pennsylvania Gazette,* and in time became a mainstay of the newspaper. While not sequential in nature, they shared a purpose essential to, though seldom associated with, the evolution of comics: social commentary. As readers became accustomed to seeing illustrated matter of a cartoon style amidst their news, it was only a matter of time before the form expanded.

The Yellow Kid was among the first recurring comic characters, one of the boys in the *Hogan's Alley* cartoon, which began appearing in the late nineteenth century. The Kid was quickly followed by characters whose names might still be familiar today, such as the Katzenjammer Kids and Mutt and Jeff. At the same time, the work of early masters like Winsor McCay (*The Rarebit Fiend* and *Little Nemo in Slumberland*) began to establish the panel

structure and standardize the codes that comics would turn into a language, as discussed at length in chapter 3 and as seen (and already subverted) in McCay's *Little Sammy Sneeze* in figure 4.2.

The wide proliferation of comic strips in newspapers was due in major part to the great print battle between Joseph Pulitzer and William Randolph Hearst, two newspaper titans of the late nineteenth and early twentieth centuries, who saw their sales increase with the inclusion of such strips and thus figured that the more strips they offered, the higher their circulations would be. The large color comic supplements available in their newspapers began creating legions of devoted fans that returned to the papers specifically for the strips themselves.

Commerce always plays a major (if not *the* major) role in the direction of cultural products. However, a crucial aspect of these strips was that they represented the first time in history an audience was exposed to the same characters in such frequent recurrence. Serialized novels within magazines had used recurring characters before, but years could pass between the end of one story and the beginning of another. And, critically, characters in serialized novels could be read about but not seen—an essential element of breeding familiarity and "intimacy" with a fictional character. Several years later, radio would create serialized dramas with characters who lived through sound and invited audiences into their lives, much as television does today. Indeed, early radio is filled with adapted comic strip and comic book characters, such as Dick Tracy, Mutt and Jeff, and Superman.

It was the comic strip that crystallized and refined the recurring character, one who people could see every week or every day, and who became as familiar as their workmates,

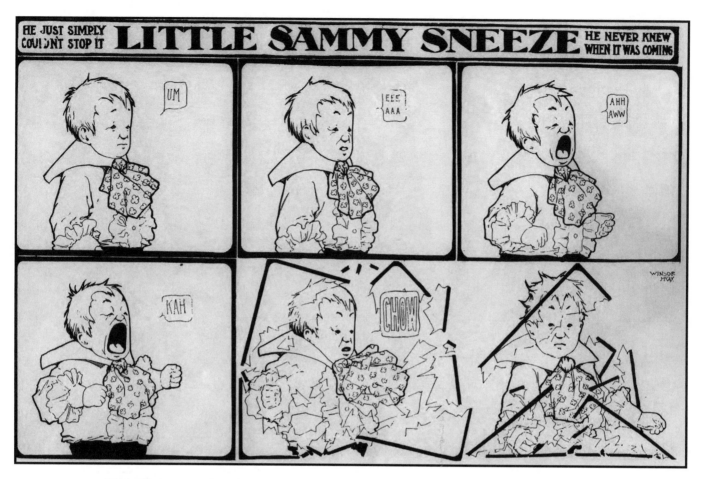

FIGURE 4.2

Little Sammy Sneeze,
by Winsor McCay

their friends, their families. Never before had popular culture begun to proliferate into people's daily lives and to occupy a place so close to the American heart.

Sensing this devotion, some astute entrepreneur (with dollar signs in his eyes, no doubt) soon realized that he could sell the strips themselves and drop the annoying news you had to wade through to get to them. The astute entrepreneur in this case was a fellow named Maxwell Gaines.

Mr. Gaines gathered a bunch of comic strips together and reprinted them in magazine form. The result was 1933's *Funnies on Parade,* considered to be the very first comic book, though it contained no original material. Shortly afterward, with the flood of young artists crowding this burgeoning art form, the first comic book of original material, *Famous Funnies,* seen with its reprint-collecting precursor in figure 4.3, was produced in 1934. With both titles selling out and turning a hefty profit, the presence of comic books was thence assured.

New titles and characters appeared instantly to capitalize on the success, though the form limited itself to what it knew: funny characters, mainly in the form of anthropomorphized animals, to appeal to young readers who were quickly becoming the primary audience. It was these comedic characters from which the form took its name: comic strips. Because pulp magazines—serialized magazine novels featuring lurid tales of adventure and mystery—were so popular at the time, detective characters also found a place within the new medium, plying their trade with the fisticuffs and gunplay that the illustrated form could dramatize to spectacular (and sometimes troubling) effect.

Comic books rode the success of established styles and character types and hauled in a decent profit. But to establish themselves in the cultural environment, comic books needed a distinct style, a character type all their own, a unique voice never heard before. They found this voice coming from a square jaw in a deep, heroic baritone, and in June 1938 the medium used this voice to change the world forever.

THE GOLDEN AGE (1938–1955)

The House that Superman Built

Masked crusaders had precedent in literature, in the likes of the Scarlet Pimpernel and Zorro (both wealthy playboys who dressed in masks and capes to fight injustice). Characters who used special powers or skills against megalomaniacal criminals had enjoyed great popularity in the late 1920s and early 1930s in the pages of the pulps, in the form of the Shadow (a wealthy playboy who dressed in a costume and cape to fight injustice). Please note that the Shadow's real name was not, as the radio would have it, Lamont Cranston. According to the source material of the pulps, Cranston was but another alias for ace pilot Kent Allard. Meanwhile, another of the pulp's great crime fighters, Doc Savage, was a veritable superman of physical and intellectual prowess. "Doc" was a nickname. The bronze hero's real name was Clark Savage Jr. Combining the first names of these two great pulp characters—Kent and Clark—reveals immediate and purposeful inspiration for what was to come.

It was, perhaps, no huge leap of imagination for two boys from Cleveland, Ohio, avid fans of such matter, to conceive of a new character that combined many of these fanciful elements. The genius of Jerry Siegel (writer) and Joe Shuster (artist) was in the way they combined it and where they put it for everyone to see.

Superman, and indeed the superhero itself (which took its name from Siegel and Shuster's creation), is a heady mixture of those pulps and adventure stories. Combined with mythological heroes, packed into an image born of circus strongmen and human cannon-balls (circus culture being a significant ingredient of entertainment culture in the 1930s), the dynamic red-and-blue figure gained huge archetypal weight. Living as we do in a world that is so aware of underlying meanings, a world where Jung's archetypes and Campbell's *Hero with a Thousand Faces* have seeped into the cultural mindscape, we can hardly imagine the impact with which such a raw, unbridled figure of the pure collective unconscious as Superman must have struck.

What finally made Superman into a figure that bore an industry and made him among the most, if not *the* most, recognizable fictional creations ever? Several vital elements of the then-contemporary social environment had been siphoned through the boys' own psychological idiosyncrasies and were caught, inadvertently, like lightning in a bottle.

Number one: Superman had a secret identity. Superman was a remarkably personal invention of the two young creators, imbued not only with their dreams but also with their obsessions, their hang-ups, their histories, and their outlooks. Like any work of art that is intensely personal, it either fails to reach any but the most rarified audience, or it catches something universal, personal to everyone in the world who sees it. While the notion of a secret identity was not unheard of, Superman's Clark Kent persona transcended what had heretofore been a simple convenience. Kent was Superman's opposed hyperbole, a sniveling boob to the invulnerable savior; not merely a means of hiding an identity, but a suit of clumsy social armor encasing an incredible, hidden strength. Clark was weak, ineffectual, and awkward (with women in particular)—powerless, in a word. But beneath the surface was strength, confidence, the ability not only to protect others, but also to be morally certain. Surely it's no mystery how such a figure would appeal to a culture of young boys, who

FIGURE 4.3

Famous Funnies 1 and *Funnies on Parade 1*.

were constantly scolded by authority figures for aggressive tendencies; boys who could feel the power inside them, but outside were awkward (with girls in particular) and ineffectual to the world of adults they saw around them. Superman was how Siegel and Shuster saw themselves. Clark Kent was how Siegel and Shuster knew everyone else saw them. And when I say Siegel and Shuster, I mean every boy alive.

Number two: Superman was an immigrant. Rocketed from the planet Krypton just as it was exploding, Superman found himself adopted by kindly parents on Earth, where he discovered that his heritage imbued him with remarkable powers that made him the superior of those he lived among. This is a common aspect of myth with clear universal appeal. Prophets like Moses and Jesus were raised by surrogate parents, and heroes like Hercules gained their great strength from their true parents who lived in the sky. In establishing who they are in the world, it is common for children to wonder if they are with their real parents, if there isn't a secret that's been hidden from them since the day they were born, and to feel that their true heritage imbues an incredible significance in them.

Superman was a metaphor beyond that, though. He represented not just a community of frustrated boys, but also another incredibly populous social group of the time: the immigrant. Siegel and Shuster were the children of Jewish immigrants themselves, living among that lifestyle and that culture. The idea of hiding a precious birthright that affords you great purpose, beneath a surface that allows you to blend in and call no undue attention to yourself, was a significant aspect of the lives the boys lived every day.

Number three: Superman was antiestablishment. Because immigrants—often poor and struggling to find work—felt they were disregarded by authority figures and were not taken into account by "the system," Siegel and Shuster put at the heart of their creation a mission of social justice. Indeed, you would hardly recognize the early Superman for the smiling, boy-scoutish authority figure we think of today. Superman was intended as a defender of the little guy, and in his first three adventures alone he battled a lynch mob, a wife beater, and a corrupt millionaire who cut corners at the expense of his employees' safety. Superman saved the falsely accused from capital punishment at the last moment, aided mistreated workers, and didn't face his first genuine mad scientist until more than a year of fighting for truth and justice. He wasn't very gentle about it either, scaring cooperation out of thugs with threats like "You see how effortlessly I crush this bar of iron in my hand? That bar could just as easily be your neck!" (Siegel 1938). Superman conformed to the methods and dialogue of the two-fisted private eyes and gumshoes of the time whose place was among the downtrodden. Thus, at its very inception the comic book offered social commentary common to young art forms, scowled at by an establishment that is being criticized, a voice for young people who felt themselves unheard.

Finally, number four: the panels were made to fit a Superman. Just as the hero had been waiting for the right medium to hold him, the medium itself was waiting for the perfect vehicle to showcase its particular strength and power. It's no accident that Siegel and Shuster failed for years to get their hero into comic strips. The shorter form and more constrained panel composition couldn't hope to contain him. Only after Siegel and Shuster had shopped their hero around for years did DC (short for *Detective Comics,* the company's flagship title) finally buy the feature—and with a shockingly bad bargain for the creators. That was neither the first nor (sadly) the last time that the business side of the industry took egregious advantage of its creators. At any rate, the comic book form proved ideally suited to the exploits of the superhero. Such incredible feats of strength and bravery needed to be visualized to have full impact. It's not enough to *say* that a person lifts a car above his head. It must be *seen* to have full effect. And so it was, in June 1938, on the cover of *Action Comics* 1, seen in figure 4.4.

FIGURE 4.4

Action Comics 1.
© DC Comics.
SUPERMAN™
DC Comics.

Because each panel of a sequence isolates an instant of action, its capacity to frame and highlight physical dynamism is exemplified. Unlike the cinema, the other visual narrative medium of the time, in comic books it didn't cost a single cent more to show a planet exploding than it did to show a man and a woman kissing (and who would want to see that, anyway?).

It was barely any time at all before the world noticed Superman. The radio, America's family pastime of the era, snatched him up in 1940, less than two years after his inception, beginning a symbiotic relationship wherein comic books supply the visualization and concept and other media catapult the property to audiences far and wide. There's little debate that comic books (and thus GNs) are the industry that Superman built. With his appearance, comic books became a ubiquitous childhood companion and pastime, and the covers and pages of comics were instantly crowded with super-imitators. No doubt the likes of Stardust the Super Wizard, Dirk the Demon, and Fero, Planet Detective, are long forgotten, perhaps deservedly so. But, as with any other art form, amidst the chaff there is that rare and beautiful wheat.

Batman followed his colorful inspiration by a year, in the May 1939 issue of *Detective Comics* (number 27 to be exact), but when he appeared, he brought several innovations with him that would prove integral to the evolution of the superhero. The creation of Bill Finger (writer) and Bob Kane (artist), Batman was really Bruce Wayne, a millionaire playboy who, as a child, saw his parents gunned down before him by a merciless criminal and consequently swore that he would have his revenge against all criminals. Bringing his wealth and his indomitable will to bear, Wayne forged himself into a weapon against crime, honing his mind and body to the peak of human ability. And do note the word *human*. Batman had no powers, but was, rather, a supremely developed human being. The force of this fantasy was hard even for a Superman to contend with: you or I or any reader could be Batman in real life, provided sufficient drive and resources.

More important still to the evolution of the form was the fact that Batman actually employed a rough, rudimentary psychology. Superman came with his mission fully formed from the instant we saw him; he intrinsically understood, like an agent of God, that his job was to use his powers for the betterment of mankind. Batman, by contrast, had something integrally human: a motive. Revenge may not be the most original, insightful, or healthy motive, but it did imbue the juvenile art form with its first inkling of emotional weight and nuance.

Batman, as it happens, also owns the dubious distinction of introducing one more trope of the form: the teen sidekick. Robin, the Boy Wonder, first appeared (in *Detective Comics* 38) less than a year after his mentor crept stealthily onto the shadowy streets of Gotham City. Intended as an audience-identification device, the sidekick may have been a flub from the very beginning. Notwithstanding the inconceivable irresponsibility, in fictional terms, of bringing young children into gun battles with psychotic murderers, the marketing theory is a weak one. Young readers were not likely to trade in the fantasy identification with the powerful and dynamic adult star of the book for that with the little twerp who had to take his orders. Batman would end up paying dearly for this induction of underage help (as would the entire comic book market) as, in a few years, the misinterpreted relationship would be among an array of charges that would alter the course of the industry.

The Holy Trinity of superheroes was completed in 1941 (in *All-Star Comics* 8) with the invention of Wonder Woman, a superpowerful Amazon from the female-inhabited Paradise Island. Her origins borrowed more overtly from mythology, as her creator, psychologist William Moulton Marston, envisioned a heroine who would strengthen the image of powerful women in the minds of young boys and open their outlooks to wider gender concerns.

Marston, as it happened, had also developed a manner of measuring blood pressure for the purpose of determining honesty, thus inventing the lie detector (two rather impressive inventions for a single lifetime). It was surely no coincidence that Wonder Woman's main weapon in her fight against crime was a golden lasso which, when wrapped around someone, would cause that person to speak the truth. Clearly, Marston's real world concerns found their way into his fantasy, and thus the social reality merged once again with the fantasy of readers throughout the country.

While this Holy Trinity, along with extremely popular characters such as the Flash and Green Lantern, was owned by DC Comics, every company around was producing their own array of supercharacters.

By 1941 World War II was our country's biggest concern and, in keeping with their established modus operandi, comic books were quick to address it. Among a veritable army of star-spangled superheroes conceived at the time, Captain America, created by industry stalwarts Joe Simon and Jack Kirby, was a standout. Armed with a red-white-and-blue shield and, yes, a young sidekick, Cap created instant controversy by punching out Adolf Hitler on the cover of *Captain America Comics* 1, in March 1941, *seven months before America had entered the war*. American involvement in the war was by no means a foregone conclusion at that point, but actually an incredibly divisive subject, and the cover, seen in figure 4.5, caused such an outcry that the Timely offices (the publishing company that would later become Marvel Comics) had to be evacuated as a result of bomb threats. Superheroes by no means began their existence as guardians of the status quo. Even the most proudly patriotic among them launched his career on a subversive note.

Paradoxically, these defenders of truth and justice did not flourish creatively during a war against darkness and evil. Writers and artists found the obvious story ideas stifling. How did you write a story that took Superman behind enemy lines and did not make the ease with which he tore down the enemy seem offensive to your average serviceman? Consequently, the boys in colorful spandex remained on our shores, battling fifth columnists and hawking war bonds for the most part. However, as a unique American artifact much treasured by servicemen on foreign shores who craved a piece of home, as well as by patriotic kids on American streets, comics reached the height of their popularity in this decade, a height it would never achieve again. The form and figures were cemented into culture, and specifically American culture, forever.

If comics were a uniquely American art form, then superheroes were their most American innovation. At a time when America was seen as the hope of the very world, an array of bright, smiling, dynamic, powerful characters would come to epitomize the country's ideal of youthful vigor and can-do, energetic confidence (some might say arrogance). With such a foothold, it's little wonder that this genre came to dominate American comics in a way no other genre would dominate any other medium, in any other country in the world.

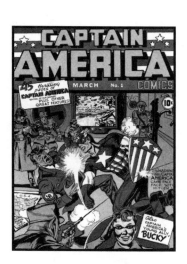

FIGURE 4.5

Captain America Comics 1.
Captain America and all other
Marvel characters: TM and
© 2010 Marvel Entertainment,
LLC, and its subsidiaries.
All rights reserved.

The Supervillain

So the superheroes did what they could for the war effort, and the war changed them forever, as it did the rest of the world. You can only wave the flag for so long before you get coopted by the Man. Sure enough, in throwing their support so wholeheartedly behind the American way, superheroes lost any hint of subversive content or critical social commentary and became staunch authority figures, guardians of the status quo who were just as likely to admonish children about listening to their parents as to smack a bank robber in the gob.

As fathers returned home from foreign shores and the American family was whole again, the culture began to show a more conservative bent as the safe, shining 1950s approached. Though they were created in 1941 as a relief from wartime angst, Archie Andrews and his gang at Riverdale High typified this distinctly optimistic outlook. *Archie* comics told the story of a squeaky-clean high school boy whose biggest problem was whether to date the gorgeous blond or the gorgeous brunette—a reductivist conceit that was surely as much an American myth as the superhero ever was. But mythology is, of course, comic books' stock in trade, and the *Archie* array of titles flourished into an empire, spawning the expected copies and paving the way for romance titles, featuring month after month of women in love with strong, honest men or women having their hearts broken by churlish, lying cads.

The humor of *Archie* and the emotional investment of the romance comics were finding an audience, even as the fantasy appeal of superhero characters remained high. But all of them were missing that certain something crucial, and a large portion of the youthful audience, perennially craving an illicit thrill in their entertainment, suddenly found a gap in their comic book life.

Enter the Gaines family once again. You may remember Max as the man who cobbled together the very first comic book out of reprinted funnies. He had, since then, founded Educational Comics in 1945. Under his son William Gaines, the company transformed into Entertaining Comics and then, finally and infamously, into EC Comics. Bill Gaines, no less astute than his father, saw the void left by the whitewashing of the superheroes and the arrival of a slightly older readership looking for harder-edged material. He formed a three-pronged publishing empire that would attract a flood of readers and eventually help shake the industry nearly apart. His true crime stories in titles such as *Crime SuspenStories* and *Shock SuspenStories,* his war stories in *Two-Fisted Tales* and *Front Line Combat* and, most renowned, his horror titles *Tales from the Crypt* (namesake of the popular television and movie series of the 1980s and 1990s), *The Vault of Horror,* and *The Haunt of Fear* set a new standard for comics in more ways than one.

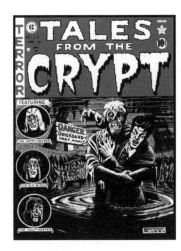

FIGURE 4.6

Tales from the Crypt 24, copyright © William Gaines, Inc., 2010, reprinted with permission.

Gaines coauthored (with Al Feldstein) most of the stories himself and acquired a stable of top-level artists, still admired today for their distinctive styles, high level of draftsmanship and realism, and powerful imagery. This alone made their titles spring out on the same racks carrying superhero and funny animal books, which at this point were beginning to show a tedious sameness in their house styles and subject matter. The artistic quality, however, was not the overt draw of the EC books. The extreme visual content, particularly in the crime and horror stories, was shocking by any account and quite intentionally so. Drug use, decomposing corpses, dismembered limbs, cannibalism, and abusive treatment of women abounded, and that was just on the covers! EC Comics did not stand alone for long. Many publishers rallied to the sensationalist and highly successful genres of crime and horror. As seen in figure 4.6, this was just the sort of thing that young boys looking for a taste of the subversive could never get enough of.

More subtly influential, perhaps, was the social commentary, which Gaines ratcheted up even by the standard of the old Superman comics. Gaines himself was a liberal-minded fellow (not the least controversial thing to be in early 1950s America) and let it show in his stories—if you could see it beneath the piles of blood-drenched corpses, that is. Woven into his tales were keen observations about racism, corruption, and social class, all of which did little to warm any authority figure to his comics. Most pronounced, though, were his depictions of war in his battle-oriented comics (see fig. 4.7), where the stories went to great lengths to depict the realistic aftermath of combat on the human psyche. With America coming out of a war whose moral overtones were clear-cut and fighting the grayer, more morally convoluted Korean conflict, few adults were keen on letting their kids "enjoy" entertainment depicting cowardly soldiers, morally compromised officers, and the overall dehumanizing effect of grim bloodshed.

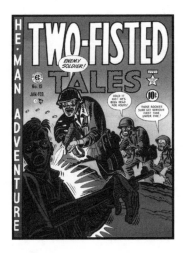

FIGURE 4.7

Two-Fisted Tales 19, copyright © William Gaines, Inc., 2010, reprinted with permission.

Far from being keen on it, in fact, they were quite furious. Comics had been entrenched in censorship battles and Senate examination as early as 1948, though they had managed to escape mainly unscathed. However, in 1954, with the rampant accusations and fear-baiting swirling about the country in the wake of Joseph McCarthy's communist witch hunts, the industry's number was up.

Even with social circumstances ripe for a cataclysm, it usually takes a person to push them over the edge. Such a person was one Frederic Wertham, a New York psychologist specializing in the treatment of children. Wertham, a trailblazer in civil rights and the humane treatment of mental illness, did not easily fit the profile of supervillain.

Having been concerned with the consequences reading comic books had for many of his young patients, Wertham began a study on the medium's effect on juveniles and compiled his "insights" in a book called *Seduction of the Innocent,* published in 1954. The sensationalism of the title had little on the accusations within, which grew from genuine seeds of concern into a claim of comics' culpability for everything from juvenile delinquency and crime to drug use, pedophilia, and even that condition so terrifying at the time as to be whispered with more cold terror than communism itself: homosexuality. Bombarded with the violent, destructive, subversive effect of comic books, the nation's defenseless youth were sure to suffer irreparably traumatized psyches.

As parent groups and government committees were already sniffing around the industry, the scholarly work of a professional psychologist was all they needed. In 1954, a Senate subcommittee was convened by Tennessee Senator Estes Kefauver to examine the effects of comic books, with the hopes of establishing government limitations on content. Wertham, naturally, served as their star witness.

The doctor detested two sorts of comics in particular. First, superhero comics, not just examples of lawless vigilantism, were also purveyors of more subtle and harmful messages. Wonder Woman was a prime example, a tough, masculine woman who often found herself chained or tied up and in the power of swarthy men with nefarious plans (read: bondage). Batman's relationship with Robin was also a major issue. The psychologist insisted on pedophiliac (not to mention homosexual) overtones in the relationship of a man and a boy in tight clothes engaging in strenuous physical activity together.

His second collection of points fell on the horror and crime comics that were typified by the product of industry leader EC. One hardly needed to look beneath the covers to horrify adults about the industry's effects on youth (if one did look beneath the covers, there was plenty more to horrify and disturb). Given that the committee and the nation had already made up their minds, by and large, Wertham's analysis had the desired effect.

Were comics of that era actually a bad influence on children? How right was Wertham? Well, Wertham's testimony (and book) was rife with misleading information. He chose only the most extreme examples and intimated that this was what all comics were filled with all the time. He took panels and events out of context. He exaggerated and misinterpreted. Wonder Woman did get tied up an awful lot in her early adventures, and whether this represented the artist's predilection for unusual sexual practices, Wertham's accusations overlooked the fact that you would really have to know what bondage was in order to draw a connection, and it's a certainty that no young Wonder Woman readers of the time had any idea about such things. Was Batman a pedophile? Clearly not. The intention was obviously to engender a sense of camaraderie that young boys would admire and recognize in their own relationships with their fathers or older brothers. In any event, no publisher with an eye toward profit (i.e., every publisher) would ever allow its heroes to be portrayed as sexually abusive to children (or, for that matter, as homosexual—not back in the 1950s, at any rate).

Horror and crime comics were a more extreme case. Their content was often sensational and violent, and it did obliterate the boundaries of what kids should be subjected to.

However, they were intended for an older audience than superhero and funny animal comics, and most of the stories used the titillating subject matter to (graphically) illustrate positive social messages—it was always the murderer who was eaten by the cannibal, always the racist who was pulled limb from limb by the zombie. These were latter-day morality tales, roughly as gruesome as Grimm's stories or some of the more intense classic fairy tales, and as such the horrific endings were reserved for the corrupt, the greedy, the spiteful.

In the end, this was really a moot question. Every new art form must face social scrutiny, disapproval, and the misinterpretation of older generations. As every generation finds its own ways to explore "forbidden" subject matter, the previous generation will always look askance at the new, more liberal art their children engage in, from comics to rock 'n' roll to video games. And, of course, a desperate, angry search for a scapegoat can turn up culprits anywhere it looks.

The industry, seeing that its days of creative freedom were numbered, scrambled to come up with a solution that would avoid direct government oversight and allow them to, in effect, censor themselves. The solution they arrived at was called the Comics Code Authority.

Every comic published was to be submitted for inspection to this authority, made up of comic book publishers and consultants from the field of education and psychology. Comics that did not meet the code's standards would not get the authority's stamp, seen in figure 4.8.

Comics that did not bear the stamp on their covers would not be distributed or carried by comic book purveyors of the day, mainly newsstands and drugstores. Of course, this was not government regulation and so publishers did not have to submit their work for inspection. But with no distribution, there were no sales and consequently no money to support your company. Failure to submit to inspection and receive a stamp was tantamount to throwing away any chances you had in the market.

The code itself was a set of strict regulations which stipulated, for instance, that authority figures (police and politicians) could never be depicted as corrupt or immoral; criminals could never be seen to win or escape in the end; and sexuality and drug use could never be depicted. As the code was developed in part by publishers, business ends took control over creative (and in this case regulatory) concerns, leading to an outrageous example of market tampering. As the story goes, the publishers saw to it that it was put into the very bylaws of the code that the words *crypt, horror,* and *fear* could not appear on the cover of any comic book. You can imagine what a fix this put industry leader EC Comics in, whose top-selling title were *Tales from the Crypt, The Vault of Horror,* and *The Haunt of Fear.* The publishers had turned the bad fortune of the code somewhat to their advantage, by running their most powerful competitor right into the ground (Mann 1988).

One of EC's titles, however, was preserved by a clever act of transformation. By putting it in magazine form, it was no longer subject to Comics Code Authority approval, and its humorous content, while irreverent, was by no means the controversy-baiting subject of horror and crime comics. The title still exists today as *Mad* magazine.

In the wake of this cataclysm, comic books settled into a conservative, parent-friendly niche, with fare limited exclusively to funny animals, prim romance, and starchy, scolding superheroes. Despite DC's effort to reinvigorate their mainstay with reimagined origins and new costumes for popular characters like Flash and Green Lantern, DC superheroes in the burgeoning Silver Age were characterized by bright, contemporary art with characters that showed a bland sameness and stories that became more and more outlandish and thus less relatable and significant. Nevertheless, it would once again be the superheroes who redefined the medium and gave it a second burst of life.

FIGURE 4.8
The Comics Code Authority stamp. © CMAA, Inc.

THE SILVER AGE (1956-1970)

Psychological Insight + Punching in the Face = Success

Marvel Comics had been languishing, in creative terms, since its character Captain America had "come home" from the war along with the rest of the country. They produced only romance comics and weird fantasy titles that played at EC's tropes, though they were banned from providing the same level of social commentary and titillating content that had given those tales their extra oomph.

In 1961, Marvel's publisher, Martin Goodman, got wind that competitor DC Comics was seeing major sales on a new title, *Justice League of America,* a title that featured DC mainstays Wonder Woman, Flash, and Green Lantern teaming up for monthly adventures with lesser-known heroes. Goodman promptly demanded that Marvel's editor in chief and head writer create a title with a similar concept (Lee and Mair 2002).

Well, Goodman's head writer was an enterprising sort who had started with Marvel as a kid, writing for *Captain America* back in the 1940s. Born Stanley Lieber, he changed his name for the byline to the somewhat more lively and memorable Stan Lee. Lee had been writing one monster story after another, struggling to come up with new creatures and new twist endings about a dozen times a month. The only thing the titles had going for them, other than Stan's snappy dialogue, was the highly individualized styles of its two artists: the potent and dynamic art of Jack Kirby (cocreator of Captain America) and the strange and striking art of Steve Ditko.

Mandated to create a superhero team with no active superheroes to draw from, Lee had to establish, in a single story, not only enough characters to form a team but the origins of their superpowers and their reason for banding together. In an inspired move, Lee created a group of four explorers who all got their powers in a single accident (a bombardment of "cosmic rays" during an experimental space flight). The genius here was the fact that their dynamic existed prior to their heroic careers, that their relationship was the reason for their bond, rather than the weak, unconvincing motive of just "doing good." With this dynamic came something vital that had been wholly absent from superheroes until now: personalities. By eschewing the stiff, bloodless character standards of the day, Lee gave birth to the Fantastic Four and, with them, the new Way of Comics for the rest of time.

As a surrogate family, the Fantastic Four's interpersonal dynamic was lively and they clashed often. They were, by turns, compassionate, argumentative, self-doubting, bitter, obsessive, loving, arrogant, kind; in short, they were just like people. The highly recognizable stable of DC heroes was differentiated primarily by costumes and (usually) powers. Beyond that, they had different professions in their secret identities and, occasionally, different hairstyles. But their faces, their dialogue, and their purposes were virtually interchangeable. The selling point for these adventures were, of course, the action and flights of fancy, not human insight or characterization. Lee's first major contribution to the form was a reversal of the most shocking sort. DC characters were superheroes who sometimes disguised themselves as normal people. Marvel's characters were normal people who sometimes dressed up as superheroes.

The emotional depth with which Lee imbued his writing was supported by his collaborator, artist Jack Kirby. Despite having been in the comic book business for more than twenty years at the time, with *Fantastic Four* Kirby introduced a whole new style to comic book art that would come to define Marvel's heroes, including a reactivated Captain America. A combination of exaggerated facial expressions that exemplified the human drama, astoundingly vital figures, and blazingly energetic movement crackling off the pages (and out of figure 4.9), its like had never been seen in comics before.

FIGURE 4.10

Amazing Spider-Man 33.
Spider-Man and all other
Marvel characters: TM
and © 2010 Marvel
Entertainment, LLC,
and its subsidiaries.
All rights reserved.

DC's artists were skilled practitioners who combined clean figural work, bright colors, and detailed urban (or futuristic if the plot called for) landscapes. In matching Lee's commitment with his own extraordinary imagination and raw craftsmanship, Kirby not only showed you the story but made you feel it, not just in the impact of a fist against a jaw, but in the emotions that Lee had put there, boiling beneath the surface.

Shooting for the moon, Lee and Kirby deepened the human element by flipping the wish-fulfillment device of superpowers, suggesting that they might not be a pure benefit for an actual human being. First on display in the Fantastic Four's resentful rock-creature superhero the Thing, this element came to full fruition in the form of the Hulk. Meek, ineffectual nuclear physicist Bruce Banner is caught in the accidental detonation of his own highly radioactive gamma bomb. Now, when he is angered, his rage transforms him into a monstrous, brutish antihero. By taking man's dual nature (weakness/strength, calm intelligence/uncontrollable rage) into account, Lee had the audacity to introduce superhero comics to their first genuine literary device: a metaphor. Undergoing a wholly unforeseen and massive emotional and intellectual growth spurt, comics acquired an actual subtext.

Lee and Kirby were on a streak. Their universe of crime fighters proliferated, each preserving the house style of humanization: Thor was a supergod who played out family politics and jealousies with a pantheon of Norse gods; Iron Man was a millionaire industrialist (and weapons dealer) who built himself a suit of high-tech armor to keep his heart beating after falling prey to a weapon of war; Captain America was pulled out of decades of suspended animation and had to deal with a confusing and ambiguous world he could never catch up with; the X-Men were a team of young heroes cursed with mutations that made them freakish even as it gave them powers, feared and hated by the world they sought to protect from other evil mutants in a reflection of the Martin Luther King/Malcolm X "by any means necessary" quandary. Titles featuring these heroes would eventually outsell their more sedate DC competition.

However, the Marvel philosophy hit its peak in what must be considered Lee's prime creation, the quintessential superhero: Spider-Man. While attending a science demonstration, socially tormented high school nerd Peter Parker is bitten by a radioactive spider and gains the spider's abilities. (There is a thesis waiting to be written on scientific phenomena in superhero origins. DC heroes, born in the 1930s and 1940s and revamped in the 1950s, were commonly products of extraterrestrial interference, the popular scientific obsession of the time. Marvel's heroes, coming to life in the 1960s, were more often than not the product of radiation gone awry, be it in the form of bombs [the Hulk], chemicals [Daredevil], or spiders, radiation having replaced aliens as the common scientific paranoia of the era. Comics once again hold a mirror up to the culture.)

The bite of a radioactive spider explains how Spider-Man became a superhero, and such abbreviated scenarios tended to be sufficient background for DC heroes. But the startling conceptual power of Spider-Man lay in the rest of his story; not how he became a superhero, but why. With a new array of superpowers, Peter does what would likely occur to most people in a similar situation: he tries to profit by them. Resentfully determined to give the world back what it had always given him—nothing—he launches a TV career, intending to look after only himself and his kindly Uncle Ben and Aunt May, the elderly couple who have raised him since the death of his parents (note the instance of yet one more orphan in the annals of the superhero). Walking out of the TV studio one evening, the newly minted Spider-Man encounters a criminal on the run from a police officer. Peter, filled with a selfish arrogance born of his new power, does not lift a finger to assist. In a karmic reversal of fortunes positively Shakespearean in scope, Peter returns home that night to find his Uncle Ben has been shot and killed by an intruder whom the police have pursued to a nearby warehouse. Peter dons his costume and invades the warehouse, tackling the killer with his enhanced strength and agility, only to find that the murderer of his beloved uncle is the same man that Peter himself allowed to escape earlier that day.

The shattered youth learns that, as his uncle always told him, "with great power must also come—great responsibility!" (Lee and Ditko 1962) Thus superpowers served as a metaphor for the pains of growing up, for the realization that, as one's power and influence increase, so must one's obligation to society.

Spider-Man proved the most human of heroes, troubled over the years by career woes, romantic complications, and his aunt's declining health. The human element of the character was exemplified by the art of Steve Ditko, whose style was the antithesis of Kirby's. Lee wisely wanted the young teenage superhero and his supporting cast to appear recognizably unheroic, and Ditko's art captured nuances of human frailty and suffering and imbued the title with a melancholy tone and a shadow-drenched atmosphere, as seen in figure 4.10, that made Spider-Man's struggles even more heroic.

Spider-Man was a watershed moment in comic history, a figure that not only epito-mized all that had come before him, but also paved the way for everything that would follow. It would be fair to say that every superhero created since is, to some extent, a reinterpreta-tion of Spider-Man. Indeed, even characters established well before him—your Supermans and Batmans—have since been recast in Spider-Man's humanized image.

Spider-Man's implications reached further still. As the more insightful level of writing in Marvel comic books attracted older readers, the teens that were now the average comic consumer found in Spider-Man a character of unequaled self-identification. Here was a teen facing much of the daily frustration that they themselves faced, and he was not the sidekick, not the second-fiddle hero. This teen was the protagonist himself and, as teen readers began to invest deeply in this character, Spider-Man did something that no other hero had ever done before (and seldom since): he grew up.

Lee followed Peter Parker's progress through high school and into college, keeping the character relevant to readers who were growing and making the same changes in their own lives. As Spider-Man's readers moved into college and on from there, the hero faced appropriate social issues, and the title steeped itself in comics' long-abandoned tradition of cultural commentary. Consideration of the Vietnam War and protests over the same, racial tensions, failing confidence in the system—all found their way into Spider-Man's adven-tures, and the hero became, to either Lee's surprise or his very canny expectations, some-thing of a counterculture icon, as evidenced by figure 4.11 (note the Comics Code Authority stamp in the upper-right-hand corner).

It was Spider-Man's countercultural status that would bring about the next major grow-ing pain in the progression of comics.

FIGURE 4.11

Amazing Spider-Man 68. Spider-Man and all other Marvel characters: TM and © 2010 Marvel Entertainment, LLC, and its subsidiaries. All rights reserved.

5

THE GRAPHIC NOVEL

WITH COMIC BOOKS A FIRMLY ESTABLISHED ELEMENT OF THE cultural landscape, we will now begin to see how they grew and matured into the GN itself. This chapter examines how the medium's elements and themes flourished in such a way as to not only expand it into a larger commercial market, but also to earn it the respect necessary to find a place in education.

THE BRONZE AGE (1971–1985)

Not Your Father's Novel

In 1970, Stan Lee was contacted by the U.S. Department of Health, which could not help but notice Spider-Man's appeal to college-age Americans, a demographic that the government was having a very hard time reaching itself. They asked Lee to write a Spider-Man story that addressed the growing problem of drug abuse, in hopes of enlightening the college crowd. Lee agreed and penned a three-issue tale that featured Peter Parker/Spider-Man's battle with his archenemy the Green Goblin, and with the drug pushers who had hooked young Harry Osborn, who happened to be not only the Green Goblin's son, but also Peter's roommate and best friend.

When Lee submitted his story to the Comics Code Authority for approval, it was, of course, immediately refused a stamp. Drugs remained an absolutely forbidden subject for comics. The irony (that the U.S. government itself had solicited this story) was not lost on Lee, and he was no doubt frustrated by the authority's refusal to allow the medium to grow with the times. Faced with a difficult decision, Lee made the most impressive choice possible: he published 1971's *Amazing Spider-Man* 96, 97, and 98 with no Comics Code Authority stamp, trusting that the popularity of the character and the title's historically high sales would convince distributors to carry the comics regardless.

His gamble paid off, and the issues sold up to their usual high standards. The foot of enlightenment had been forced into the door of comic book censorship and would not easily be removed again. Indeed, over at DC Comics, writer Denny O'Neil and artist Neal Adams were taking the conservative Green Lantern and the liberal Green Arrow on a road trip through America's tumultuous social landscape. In the wake of Lee's Spider-Man story, O'Neil and Adams produced *Green Lantern/Green Arrow* 85 and 86 (both 1971), in which we learn that Green Arrow's teen sidekick, Speedy, has become a heroin junkie.

Concurrent to this drama, a new breed of comic book was being born. Available not in the standard venues, but rather in head shops, counterculture bookstores, and the dorm rooms of the guys who always had the best pot, underground comics (also called *comix*) depicted a world of druggy euphoria, social and political dissatisfaction, and raunchy sexual humor that comics had never seen before. Needless to say, the Comics Code Authority had no involvement in this end of the business.

Produced by fringe artists, mainly in San Francisco, figures like Robert Crumb and characters like the Fabulous Furry Freak Brothers were beginning to entertain an adult audience with a much different agenda than your average superhero readership. Both on the official and unofficial fronts, comic books were poised for an evolutionary advancement.

By the early 1970s, the medium was slowly proving it could appeal to the sensibilities of adults, and comics began dallying with a new format, one that would put them in a more profitable position than on comic book racks and newspaper stands: on bookstore shelves. A handful of works, describing themselves with near misses like "illustrated comics novel," came along in the fantasy, sci-fi, and mystery genres, often mixing sequential page composition with more "acceptable "prose narrative. Lee and Jack Kirby took a crack at it, maintaining the word balloons, with an adventure of their counterculture space hero, the Silver Surfer, in 1978.

Will Eisner was pivotal in defining the language of sequential art with his Golden Age character the Spirit, much the way Orson Welles established the cinematic language in *Citizen Kane*. It is Eisner who must be credited with producing the first graphic novel per se. The name *graphic novel,* like the term *sequential art* itself, was Eisner's invention. Released in 1978, *A Contract with God and Other Tenement Stories* was also the first sequential work available in bookstores that contained original material of a nongenre nature and that was specifically intended for adults. As a book, it was absolutely not subject to Comics Code scrutiny. The work, about Jewish tenement life in the 1920s, proved enough of a success that other publishers took notice. Marvel and DC began experimenting with reprints of popular superhero material and then original material in the new format, though with the fitful commitment of a business that doesn't completely believe what it's doing will work. Nevertheless, more than just a foot had been pushed in the door this time, and very quickly; creators with serious artistic agendas—many of whom had grown up reading comic books— began to see the form's expanding potential.

THE MODERN AGE (1986–PRESENT)

Down to Business

The year 1986 is widely considered to be the year that changed comics. First up was Art Spiegelman's format-defining *Maus,* which began life in 1973 in underground comics and finally came into its collected and well-known form thirteen years later. *Maus* focused on a son's emotional reckoning with his aging father, as the father recollects his family's trials during the Nazi occupation of Poland and internment in the Auschwitz concentration camp. Using the primal comic book device of the anthropomorphized animal to have cats stand in for Nazis and mice for Jews, *Maus* not only had literary themes at its heart but also served as both a subversive comment on the medium's past and an example of what its future could be. It was shocking, powerful, insightful, and highly unexpected. Recipient of much well-deserved acclaim and media attention, it was the first (and only) graphic novel to be awarded a Pulitzer Prize (a special presentation in 1992) and has since become the only graphic novel that reliably and consistently turns up in school curricula.

The year 1986 had two other major surprises as well. Both collected from serialized monthly issues, *Dark Knight Returns* and *Watchmen* pushed the superhero genre light years ahead in terms of maturity and sophistication of content. The former, written and illustrated by Frank Miller, told of an aging Batman's return to crime fighting in a future Gotham City ravaged by crime and governmental neglect. As much a social satire as a superhero adventure, the book's intellectual considerations and bone-crunching violence were unprecedented in mainstream comics and clearly the work of a man who intended to offer adults a message of some significance.

More ambitious still was Alan Moore and Dave Gibbons's genre-redefining deconstruction of the superhero in *Watchmen.* Set in an alternate world where Nixon is still president and superheroes have been outlawed, it details the hunt for a serial killer of former crime fighters, a hunt that forces a number of retired superheroes out of lives of quiet desperation. *Watchmen* was dense, cerebral, and extremely disturbing in its exploration of what "real" superheroes would be like. Much as Spider-Man had given the superhero a human dimension, the characters in *Watchmen* pushed it into the realm of literary tragedy. These "heroes" were vain, homicidal, suicidal, drug-addicted, pathetic, sexually frustrated, aberrant, and impotent, and their situation was intended to reflect the effect that such awesome responsibility would have on actual human psyches, as well as what a superpowered being would mean in terms of actual world politics, diplomacy, and the economy. One of very few sequential works that could safely be called graphic literature, *Watchmen* is the only graphic novel on *Time* magazine's 100 greatest novels from 1923 to 2005 and is still considered a high-water mark in the field.

Dark Knight Returns and *Watchmen* were the first superhero-oriented works to be reviewed in the mainstream media and took that huge final step toward making the superhero genre "respectable" enough that such content might wind up in the hands of nonenthusiasts.

It is worth noting that these three GNs—*Maus, Dark Knight Returns,* and *Watchmen,* the three books that put the GN on the map in terms of mainstream recognition and acceptance—all began as serialized sequential art works and were only later collected into the GN form in which they earned notoriety.

Since 1986, GNs have gathered steam and barreled ahead, becoming a standard fixture of the market. Even as GNs were making their way into bookstores, comic books themselves had a new venue, in the comic book specialty shop. Stores devoted to sales of comics and comic-related items (figures, posters, T-shirts) had taken over from drugstores and news-stands. Such stores have proven an excellent repository of the widest array of sequential art material available and are still the best bet for finding more obscure works.

The industry's leading publisher, Marvel Comics, experienced a major shakeup in 1992 when several of its most popular artists broke off and formed their own company, Image Comics. Image, along with several other independent publishers, including the horror- and crime-leaning Dark Horse Comics, could not disrupt Marvel and DC's hold on the market share too badly. However, the independent publishers have managed to open the comic book market to a much wider array of genres and interests and have done a great deal to upset the nigh unbreakable headlock that superheroes have on the medium. DC Comics, which ironically became the far more experimental of the two big publishers, conceived its Vertigo imprint, which published more daring fare and is responsible for such critically acclaimed works as *Unwritten, Y: The Last Man,* and *Fables.* DC's 2011 foray into a full scale digital program continues to expand the medium's possibilities.

The underground sensibility has bloomed into the alternative comics scene, where artists whose creative agenda would once have seemed bizarre for mass comics consumption now brought an entirely new perspective and aesthetic to the table. Creators like Daniel Clowes (*Ghost World*), Harvey Pekar (*American Splendor, The Quitter*), and Chris Ware (*Jimmy Corrigan: The Smartest Kid on Earth*) have redefined GNs for the market and the culture.

Submitting work to the Comics Code Authority, once voluntary only in name, has become a far less frequent occurrence. DC and Marvel, along with most independent publishers, have opted for a set of parent advisory labels devised in-house. The code, once the scourge of the industry, is now all but dead.

As comic books and GNs have expanded into mainstream view, movie studios have been eager to latch onto popular characters that lend themselves to cinematic expansion. The smashing success of movies like *Spider-Man, Iron Man,* and *Dark Knight* prove that superheroes still resonate along mythological lines that have universal appeal. These movies serve, as radio did once upon a time, to expand recognition and acceptance of the comic book format itself. Witness Disney's 2009 purchase of Marvel Comics, based on the comic company's towering market potential. Movies based on such nonsuperhero GNs as *Ghost World* and *American Splendor* have met with critical and box office success as well.

Thanks in no small part to this cinematic boost and to comics publishers' practice of regularly reprinting story arcs of their major titles into trade GN collections, the market power of the GN is no longer debatable. Between 2000 and 2006, GN sales rocketed from $75 million to $330 million, a boost in sales nearly unprecedented in the publishing industry (Thompson 2007).

Major book publishers have recognized the potential of the GN and launched efforts such as Roaring Brook's high-quality First Second imprint that publish writers and artists whose aesthetic outlook may have been formed from childhood affection for comics but whose artistic concerns and sensibilities are a mile away from the standard fare. Artists like Alison Bechdel (*Fun Home*), Marjane Satrapi (*Persepolis*), David Small (*Stitches,* National Book Award nominee), Craig Thompson (*Blankets*), and Gene Yang (*American Born Chinese,* the first GN to be nominated for a National Book Award) have produced works of artistic integrity and profound human insight without a single costumed crime fighter among them.

These artists are leading the format further down the path that has already gained it widespread acceptance. In a deep irony, a medium that began existence as a pastime for children, was watered down by government scrutiny, and then had to earn acceptance in adult circles has only recently been able to return to its roots—in the hands of children—and into the unexplored country of school libraries.

PART THREE

Annotated Reading Lists

THE INTENTION OF THESE LISTS IS STRAIGHTFORWARD: TO create the most well-rounded collection possible with the most interesting, educational, and enjoyable books featuring the best storytelling and art. I have included books from a wide range of genres and talent that focus on a variety of subjects pertinent to each age group. The list is arranged by grade level, and each entry includes applicable genres and discussion topics for classroom use. If you are looking to fill in a collection, highlight certain areas, experiment with the possibilities of the format, or develop a specialized collection for a curriculum or classroom, the list here is a good starting point. (Also see the index of discussion topics for titles by discussion topic.)

This is all with the understanding that the format handles some areas better than others, specializing in certain genres, ignoring others completely. Fiction is heavily weighted, though where one variety is apt to dominate I have tried to choose examples that effectively crosspollinate the genres. The following genres are included:

adventure	humor	realistic fiction
biography	literary adaptation	science fiction
fairytale/folktale	mythology	superhero
fantasy	nonfiction	war and consequences
horror		

Still the most common figures in the format, superheroes are often met with a great deal of suspicion among educators. By eschewing them completely, however, you are crucially weakening your collection. Superheroes remain a powerful metaphor for children and young adults. There are some themes (responsibility, for instance) that the genre still handles better than anything else in the format, and many superhero titles give significant issues very intelligent and balanced handling. I've integrated many of the superhero titles under other genres, but where they are not, I urge you to look closely before dismissing them. Some have an garish appearance but may well be more accessible (and educational) to your young readers than to yourself.

The lists are broken down by grade level: preschool through grade 8 in chapter 6, grades 9 through 12 in chapter 7. The titles in each grade-level section are listed alphabetically by the author's last name (or by title when necessary). Grade-level recommendations are not based on reading level exclusively, but also on thematic content. Needless to say, the recommendations are made with an imagined composite child in mind, a child culled from pedagogical theory and my own experience with children. Every book should ultimately be judged on an individual basis when possible. My suggestions are no substitute for your own knowledge of your readers and for getting to know the books on your own.

Following each annotation is a list of discussion topics (see text box) that can be used to relate to particular areas of the curriculum or to talk about informally.

DISCUSSION TOPICS

Each annotated GN is accompanied by a list of discussion topics for curricular or classroom use. For a list of the GN titles by discussion topic, please consult the index.

Art history. An adaptation or close examination of historical works. The specific area examined is listed parenthetically (comics, dance, literature, visual).

Arts. An unusual statement on the arts or techniques beyond standard sequential art repertoire. Specific art is listed parenthetically (dance, literature, music, visual).

Careers. Development of skills for a career and strategies for entering the job market.

Coming-of-age. How a young character acquires wisdom essential to maturity.

Dating and relationships. Dating at its beginning stages and the formation of romantic relationships.

Drug use. Use and abuse of addictive drugs.

Family issues. Family dynamics and the effects of divorce.

Gender roles. Expectations of social behavior based on gender, predominantly for females, including the evolution and subversion of these expectations.

Illness. Physical and emotional effects of physical afflictions.

Language arts. Early literacy development and skills for understanding and interpreting images (includes wordless GNs).

Life skills. Taking responsibility, working with others, friendship; issues of alienation, peer pressure, and group dynamics (particularly within school environments).

Mental health. Emotional disorders such as depression and schizophrenia.

Physically challenged. Features a physically challenged character.

Politics. How governments work and the ideologies underlying them, as well as issues of civil disobedience, conflict resolution, and privacy.

Popular culture. Effects of media and popular culture on modern life.

Prejudice. Bias based on race, ethnicity, or cultural status.

Racial/ethnic identity. Development of a sense of self, based in race or ethnicity; features characters of color in strong roles.

Religion. Religious beliefs and choices.

Science and technology. Scientific and mechanical instruction.

Sexual orientation. Choices about homosexuality and lesbianism.

Sexuality. Emotional and physical effects of emerging sexuality, including body changes and sexual intercourse; for grades 9–12, contains elements of sexuality in the narrative.

Socioeconomic class. Financial position in society.

Terrorism. Acts of terrorism and their effects.

U.S. history. Specific events in the country's history and cultural evolution.

War. Causes and effects of war, and events during war (actual or fictional).

World history. Specific events in the history of the world and the cultural evolution of other countries.

For a few rare entries, I have noted that a book is out of print. I have included very few of these and only when the book in question is such a classic of the field or of such high quality that I feel it's worthwhile pursuing through the numerous online used bookseller inventories (when I last checked, Amazon.com could provide every one of the out-of-print choices).

Note that the lists in chapters 6 and 7 contain twenty-four titles that are accompanied by an asterisk (*). These are the cream of the crop, the absolute top of the form and if your budget (or interest) is limited, you can build a solid, tight, well-rounded collection with just this relatively small group of books.

A reading list is the most transitory component of a book like this. New and worthwhile GNs that belong in a pedagogical environment are released every week, and no list can replace a visit to the local bookstore or comic book store to peruse the latest choices. However, many titles listed here are already considered classics, and that will never change. Many others are—for my money—future classics. At best, the titles here will provide a guideline for constructing your own powerful and flexible reading lists in the future.

6

Annotated Reading Lists
PRESCHOOL THROUGH GRADE 8

THE TITLES BELOW COVER A BROAD RANGE OF THEMES AND discussion topics, which is a tribute to the form's great advantage: the use of words and pictures to support each other in conveying complex ideas that might be more difficult for prose or the standard picture-book format to put across in an age-appropriate way.

There are, however, a few picture books with a sequential form on the list below, mainly at the younger end. Picture books have borrowed the language of comics for far longer than other media and offer an unusual but powerful hybrid of the two. And as with the picture book itself, you can move along this list and watch how bright colors and movement start to give way to more subtle artistic expression, to match the interests and capabilities of growing readers.

PRESCHOOL-GRADE 1

Briggs, Raymond. *The Snowman*. Random House, 1999.

Genre: fantasy
Discussion Topics: language arts, life skills

The children's classic and, possibly, the first picture book ever to employ a sequential narrative. A young boy builds a snowman that comes to life and takes him on a remarkable journey.

Charming art brimming with character and warmth and a masterful sequential page composition fill this wordless story with a sense of tranquility and wonder, and a touch of melancholy.

Casper the Friendly Ghost 60th Anniversary Special. Dark Horse, 2009.

Genre: humor
Discussion Topics: art history (comics), language arts, life skills

Despite the dictates of other ghosts, young Casper refuses to scare people, choosing instead to befriend the kind and innocent even as he unintentionally foils the plans of various meanies.

Casper proves an ideal reader-identification figure with his dogged, but good-natured determination to do things his way. Packed with an array of stories (both sequential and prose) featuring the friendly ghost as well as less-known characters, the pages are saturated with the deep yellow of the original Golden Age material, offering young readers an opportunity to discover the magic of the old comics.

Cosentino, Ralph. *Batman: The Story of the Dark Knight.* Viking, 2008.

Genre: superhero
Discussion Topics: art history (comics), language arts

An overview of the caped crusader's mission to forge himself into a weapon against crime and protect the streets of Gotham City from such fiendish criminals as the Joker and Two-Face.

The deep shadowed blacks and art deco style imbue this picture book with a startling atmosphere seldom found in offerings for this age group. Narrated by Batman himself, the book passes over the tragic elements of his origin (the death of his parents) quickly and vaguely and highlights his resolve to better himself. This is just the book to satisfy young readers' cravings for superhero action while offering an unusually high degree of artistic quality. The same quality of craft and style has been applied to Cosentino's companion pieces, *Superman: The Story of the Man of Steel* and *Wonder Woman: The Story of the Amazon Princess*.

O'Connor, George. *Kapow!* Aladdin, 2007.

Genre: realistic fiction, superhero
Discussion Topics: family issues, gender roles, language arts, life skills, racial/ethnic identity

Two young playmates gallivant about the house, living the adventures of American Eagle and Bug Lady. But when there's an unexpected accident, the young would-be superheroes learn an important lesson about truth and responsibility.

The story of the two children alternates with dynamic pictures of their fantasy characters in grand adventures. This homage to the great superhero comics and a child's imagination also spares the pedantry for an age-appropriate lesson about taking responsibility for your own actions.

Slade, Christian. *Korgi.* **Top Shelf Productions, 2007.**

Genre: fantasy
Discussion Topics: gender roles, language arts, life skills

The Mollies are a mystical, forest-dwelling race, something of a cross between hobbits and fairies. Ivy, a Mollie girl, and her Korgi companion Sprout, a puppy-cute canine creature that can breathe fire, run afoul of the nearby forest monsters and escape by the skin of their wings.

The fine-lined, black-and-white illustrations are detailed, fluid, and energetic and depict the gorgeous forests and monster caves with exquisite precision. With no words, the story is still as archetypal an adventure as you can find about community and friendship.

*Spiegelman, Art, and Francoise Mouly. Toon Books series.
TOON Books, 2008–.

Genre: humor, realistic fiction
Discussion Topics: family issues, gender roles, language arts, life skills, racial/ethnic identity

GN luminary Spiegelman (*Maus*) and Mouly have taken their deep commitment to the art form and channeled it into a series of books filled with high-quality art and simple, powerful, fun narratives. Sequential art is classically difficult to read out loud, but here are classic childhood themes and story elements told with a fresh perspective and a heaping helping of creative panache that adults can easily share with young readers.

Contributing writers and artists are culled from children's literature, comic book history (even from the world of underground comix), and the ranks of new talent, and all the titles are spot-on to clue the youngest audiences into the fun of the format. Two standouts are *Otto's Orange Day* by Frank Cammuso and Jay Lynch, about a cat with a maniacal love for the color orange and a troublesome genie who grants his orange-tinted wish, and *Benny and Penny in Toybreaker* by Geoffrey Hayes, about a brother and sister who have to deal with a rough toy-breaking cousin.

KINDERGARTEN–GRADE 2

Feiffer, Jules. *Meanwhile . . . .* **HarperCollins, 1999.**

Genre: adventure
Discussion Topics: family issues, language arts, life skills

A young boy uses the magic word *meanwhile* to escape chores and adventure his way through pirate duels, cowboy chases, and space battles.

Master cartoonist Feiffer, who started his cartooning career under Will Eisner, crafts a deconstructionist take on the sequential art form at the same time that he pays homage to the wild, wonderful power of imagination.

Shepard, Aaron. *Master Man: A Tall Tale of Nigeria.*
HarperCollins, 2000.

Genre: fairy tale/folktale
Discussion Topics: family issues, life skills, racial/ethnic identity

The strongest man in his village, Shadusa insists that his wife call him Master Man, despite her admonitions that, no matter how strong you are, there's always someone stronger. Sure enough, Shadusa is shortly on the run from a towering, elephant-eating giant named Master Man. The pursuit runs them smack into another foul-tempered, massive-muscled giant named . . . Master Man!

   Though now out of print, this is an instantly accessible story of pride going before the fall, with battling titans sure to crack the shell of even the most resistant boys. David Wisniewski's art brings this picture book with sequential page composition to a whole new level, using paper cutouts that give the environment depth and allows the powerful African characters to leap from the page.

GRADES 1-3

Czekaj, Jef. *Grampa and Julie: Shark Hunters.* **Top Shelf Productions, 2004.**

Genre: humor
Discussion Topics: family issues, gender roles, language arts, life skills, science and technology

Julie and her grandfather set off to find Stephen, the world's largest shark. Looking for a shark leads to many adventures, including, naturally enough, pirates. But, appropriate to Czekaj's delightful sense of the absurd, the two also find their way to Antarctica and outer space. Also features the coolest grandmother ever.

   Ridiculous humor spot-on for the age group matches whimsical, off-kilter pictures to produce a work that modernizes the hilarity and whimsy of the early Sunday comic strips.

Graphic Spin Fairy Tales series. Stone Arch Books, 2008–.

Genre: fairy tale/folktale
Discussion Topics: language arts

Stone Arch Books has put the classics into GN form in their Graphic Spin imprint, remaining true to the story but giving a contemporary look and energy to the art. This is a great way for young readers to see stories they're already familiar with in a new way. This familiarity can support early literacy education, luring new readers in and helping them build confidence.

   For a full list of titles, visit www.stonearchbooks.com, but *Cinderella* (by Beth Bracken and Jeffrey Stewart Timmins), *Hansel and Gretel* (by Donald Lemke and Sean Dietrich), and *Red Riding Hood* (by Martin Powell and Victor Rivas) are three of the best.

Lechner, John. *Sticky Burr: Adventures in Burrwood Forest.* **Candlewick, 2008.**

Genre: adventure
Discussion Topics: life skills, science and technology

Burrs are those spiky plants that stick to pants and shoes when you walk through forests. Sticky Burr is one of the nice ones. He isn't looking to cause anybody trouble, and his thoughtful consideration of problems has gotten his village out of difficult situations before. Partially due to the rabble-rousing Scurvy Burr, Sticky has to make a quick escape from town, but he returns just in time to save the village from an attack by wild dogs, with the help of friendly fireflies. A second adventure, *The Prickly Peril,* follows.

The popping, cartoon-style art and snappy dialogue keep the adventure moving at a good clip. The story is interspersed with a nature journal that illustrates various insects, forest dangers, and sticky situations a burr can get into.

Runton, Andy. Owly series. Top Shelf Productions, 2004–.

Genre: adventure
Discussion Topics: language arts, life skills

In five volumes, Runton's tales of the warm-hearted owl have taken solid hold in GN collections. Tackling universal subjects like fear, sacrifice, judging by appearance, failure, and, above all, friendship, these stories are powerfully affecting for their apparent simplicity. Helping a worm find his home, helping a hummingbird rescue his friend, helping others learn to fly, or welcoming newcomers to the forest, Owly proves himself the gentlest, most innocent, and most compassionate of characters.

Runton has mastered the ability to capture moods within sequential composition, and his use of the form is the most subtly complex in books for this age range. Take note, however, that although these predominantly silent stories—rendered in a warm and cartoon-classical style—appear easy for the youngest readers to follow, they often feature icons and symbols that create relatively complex sequences.

Spiegelman, Art, and Francoise Mouly, eds. *TOON Treasury of Classic Children's Comics.* **TOON Books, 2009.**

Genre: humor
Discussion Topics: art history (comics), language arts

A massive chunk of comic book, compiling the works of various early luminaries of the field, from the 1940s to the 1960s. There's a little bit of everything here, from the well-known (Dennis the Menace, Little Lulu, Donald Duck, and Captain Marvel) to the obscure (Egghead Doodle, the Tweedle Twins, and Patsy Pancake), sorted into five chapters: "Hey, Kids!" "Funny Animals," "Fantasyland," "Story Time!" and "Wacky and Weird." No other book offers such a great variety of material.

GRADES 2-4

Debon, Nicolas. *The Strongest Man in the World: Louis Cyr.*
Groundwood Books, 2007.

Genre: biography
Discussion Topics: careers, family issues, world history

Real-life Canadian circus strongman Cyr recounts his rise to fame and his feats of epic strength to his young daughter on the eve of his retirement.

Cyr apparently was the strongest man in the world when he rose to prominence in the late nineteenth century, lifting an astonishing 2,371 pounds to claim the title. Such a character has obvious allure for young readers, and Debon's pale-toned, delicate sequential art is both evocative of the time and the perfect medium for recounting the exploits of a man with superstrength.

Graphic Revolve Mythology series. Stone Arch Books, 2009–.

Genre: mythology
Discussion Topics: religion, world history

Like Stone Arch's Graphic Spin imprint that handles fairy tales, its Graphic Revolve imprint does a great job capturing the classically heroic deeds and scale while making the look and narrative feel fresh and modern for potentially jaded readers.

A full list of titles is available at www.stonearchbooks.com, but not surprisingly, the biggest heroic deeds fit best into the panels of these pages. The most standout adaptations are *Perseus and Medusa* (by Blake A. Hoena), *Jason and the Golden Fleece* (by Nel Yomtov), and *The Adventures of Hercules* (by Martin Powell).

Hatke, Ben. *Zita the Spacegirl.* **First Second, 2011.**

Genre: science fiction
Discussion Topics: gender roles, language arts, life skills

When her friend Joseph is sucked through an interdimensional portal, Zita plunges after him and winds up on the most bizarre planet this side of a Star Wars cantina. Collecting an array of zany alien allies, she courageously fights her way to Joseph and a new understanding of responsibility.

Hatke imbues his adventure with a sense of wonder even as he gives Zita's emotional journey real weight. His cartooning is charming, and his inventions are as whizbang as any young reader could want, while Zita herself is a realistically can-do heroine with lessons to learn that fans of Ramona Quimby will recognize and love.

*Holm, Jennifer. Babymouse series. Random House, 2005–.

Genre: humor
Discussion Topics: family issues, gender roles, language arts, life skills

Babymouse is your average adventure-seeking, popularity-craving, friend-loving, mischief-making, daydreaming, nine-year-old mouse. Over the course of the series, she is driven by her exuberant flights of fancy into everything from putting on a musical, conquering the dodgeball field, and figuring out a Halloween costume to ice-skating, surfing, racing cars, and joining the math club. Best friend Wilson, archnemesis Felicia Furry Paws, and irritating little brother Squeak come along for the ride and variously offer support and trouble for the intrepid and reader-identifiable heroine.

One of the trailblazers of graphic novels for younger children, Babymouse is a series that can legitimately be called delightful. Its frenetic, pink-toned art gives the narrative an appealingly manic energy. The themes (family, popularity, friendship, imagination) will be immediately accessible to readers, and the ambitious, sometimes prickly, always hyper-imaginative heroine with frustratingly uncontrollable whiskers often manages to learn (and teach) a lesson or two, despite herself. Pure, unadulterated fun.

Nobleman, Mark Tyler. *Boys of Steel: The Creators of Superman.* Knopf, 2008.

Genre: biography
Discussion Topics: art history (comics), careers, family issues, popular culture

The story of Superman's creators in picture book form. An examination not only of how the young sons of Jewish immigrants came up with the industry-defining idea, but also of the difficulties of their later lives and the struggle for creator's rights in the comic book business.

Nobleman captures the factors in Siegel and Shuster's early lives that led to the creation of the first superhero and, in back matter, discusses how they were taken advantage of, all in an engaging and age-appropriate package.

*Sturm, James. *Adventures in Cartooning: How to Turn Your Doodles into Comics.* First Second, 2009.

Genre: adventure, humor
Discussion Topics: arts (visual), gender roles, language arts, life skills

An eager knight, a horse with a sweet tooth, and a magic elf go after a gum-chewing dragon and, in the pursuit, elucidate the rudiments of sequential art, from common iconography and terminology to panels and word balloons.

As much a how-to as a postmodern fairy tale adventure, this book will satisfy those who are looking for a great story loaded with fun and a surprising girl-powered twist as well as those who are looking for a primer in the sequential art basics. The creative team also plays with panel size and page composition to keep the visuals as engaging and vigorous as the story.

Varon, Sara. *Robot Dreams.* First Second, 2007.

Genre: fantasy
Discussion Topics: language arts, life skills

A dog receives a robot companion in the mail, but after some quality time together, the robot appears to break down. Separated, the dog pines for his friend, and the robot, conscious but immobile, dreams of happier times and possibilities. Eventually they both manage to move on, but they are forever changed by their friendship.

A remarkably complex array of emotions comes across in this silent paean to friendship and longing. Varon's ability to convey layered meanings in pictures is masterful.

GRADES 3-5

Hoena, B. A. *Matthew Henson: Arctic Adventurer*. Capstone Press, 2006.

Genre: biography
Discussion Topics: careers, prejudice, racial/ethnic identity, science and technology, world history

The story of the courageous and resourceful Henson, a real-life Indiana Jones of sorts, from a childhood being forced into demeaning jobs because of his race, to his travels with Admiral Robert Peary and their discovery of the North Pole.

Solid, straightforward art keeps the amazing story popping right along. The book includes biographical and historical background. It is sure to fascinate and, more important, inspire.

Krosoczka, Jarrett J. Lunch Lady series. Knopf Books, 2009–.

Genre: adventure
Discussion Topics: careers, gender roles, socioeconomic class

Supersecret crime buster Lunch Lady serves up the "whamburgers" to robot-building science teachers, a cabal of video game–destroying librarians, and summer camp swamp creatures with the help of various lunch-themed gadgets (helicopter spatula, anyone?).

These school-centered adventures turn a familiar figure surely taken for granted by most kids (the lady who serves up the hot meals in the cafeteria) into an unlikely hero. Fans of Babymouse will have no trouble jumping aboard this one.

Sava, Scott Christian. *Hyperactive*. Idea and Design Works, 2008.

Genre: adventure, humor
Discussion Topics: family issues, language arts, popular culture

When Joey Johnson discovers that he's acquired superspeed, he gets down to the business of taking care of household chores. However, a corporate CEO has set his sights on Joey's super-DNA, and when everything from sports-drink companies to the mafia gets into the game, Joey and his family are embroiled in a hilarious adventure.

Sava uses the visual style, popping-bright colors, and the wacky but knowing humor from popular cartoons like *Spongebob Squarepants* to freshen up the archetypal tropes of the superhero origin myth and make it irresistible for a new generation.

Schade, Susan. *The Fog Mound*. Vol. 1: *The Travels of Thelonious*. Aladdin, 2007. Vol. 2: *Faradawn*. Aladdin, 2008. Vol. 3: *Simon's Dream*. Aladdin, 2009.

Genre: adventure, science fiction
Discussion Topics: gender roles, language arts, life skills, politics, prejudice, war

Young Thelonious Chipmunk dreams of adventure and wonders about the time before animals could speak and were sovereign creatures, the time when Man still existed. Thelonious is swept away by a flood and winds up in the Ruined City, where he meets several companions, including a porcupine librarian, a helicopter-flying bear, and a lizard criminal.

Together, they escape the clutches of the Dragon Lady and her ratmink flunkies and make their way toward the legendary Fog Mound, where the secrets of Man's disappearance might be found. Over the course of the trilogy, they meet a menagerie of supporting players, including a mute (and miniature) human scientist who holds the clues to the overall mystery. Before they have their answers, though, they are caught in the giant battle between an army of giant lobsters and the Dragon Lady's forces.

Alternating chapters of sequential art and illustrated prose, this book is an excellent tool for literacy development, on top of being a thrilling and surprisingly complex adventure. Employing elements of *Watership Down, The Wizard of Oz,* and *Planet of the Apes,* this multivolume adventure will feel truly epic to young readers, even as it defines each character cleverly and engagingly and offers some serious material to chew on about the environment and the consequences of shortsightedness.

Spiegelman, Art, and Francoise Mouly, eds. *Big Fat Little Lit.* Puffin, 2006. *Little Lit: Folklore and Fairy Tale Funnies.* RAW Junior, 2000. *Little Lit: It Was a Dark and Silly Night . . .* RAW Junior, 2003. *Little Lit: Strange Stories for Strange Kids.* RAW Junior, 2001.

Genre: fairy tale/folktale, humor
Discussion Topics: arts (visual), language arts

Spiegelman and Mouly gather an astonishing array of international, alternative, and literary talents in books that capture all the intricate possibilities of the form and tell an array of stories that range from the hilariously wacky to the deeply strange, from the powerfully thoughtful to the downright subversive (in the best way possible), and encompass everything from retold fairy tales to newly conceived flights of astonishing (and sometimes disturbing) imagination.

An amazing and unprecedented roster of talent has produced what may actually be children's comics' greatest artistic achievement to date. There is truly something here for every taste, and much to challenge preconceived notions of what can be done with the form. The three original volumes (*Folklore and Fairy Tale Funnies,* focusing on retold folktales and fairy tales and on stories told in a folktale and fairy tale style; *Strange Stories for Strange Kids,* focusing on weird, fantastical and often surreal stories; and *It Was a Dark and Silly Night . . . ,* focusing on humorous tales), are all out of print, though a selection from all three is available in *Big Fat Little Lit.*

Thompson, Jill. *Magic Trixie* series. HarperCollins, 2008–.

Genre: fantasy
Discussion Topics: family issues, gender roles, life skills

Being the daughter of a good-natured witch and warlock may give you pink hair, but it doesn't make it any easier to have a baby sister or come up with something for show and tell. Trixie is filled with spirit and knows just enough magic to get into trouble, and whether she's having a sleepover with werewolves, mummies, and vampires or figuring out how to turn a dragon back into her little sibling, Trixie and her very patient parents feature in clever, solid stories.

Unless witches are a problem, there is nothing in these charming, family- and school-oriented stories that could possibly read as offensive, and the hip, stylish art makes the books stand out from the crowd.

GRADES 4-6

Gownley, Jimmy. Amelia Rules series. Atheneum, 2004–.

Genre: realistic fiction
Discussion Topics: family issues, gender roles, life skills

At the ripe old age of nine, Amelia is the grand dame of tween GNs, a true trailblazer for the demographic, by including powerful and important content. Fourth grader Amelia, her friends Reggie and Pajamaman, and her archnemesis Rhonda tackle crucial childhood issues such as the holidays, superheroes, and ninjas, but also face moving to new neighborhoods, defining friendships, living with single parents, and reconciling divorce in their own young lives.

The volumes in this series are filled with short vignettes that flesh out a world that is the tonal legacy of Peanuts: filled with friends and games, but one where the melancholy of life also has a place. Gownley writes with the heart of a nine-year-old himself and creates humorous fun that stops the heavier elements from weighing it down and keeps everything in the proper, childcentric perspective.

Hergé. The Adventures of Tintin series. Little, Brown, 1929–1986.

Genre: adventure
Discussion Topics: life skills, politics, war, world history

Originally produced as a comic strip by Belgian master Hergé in 1929, the young, world-traveling reporter Tintin and his dog, Snowy, more or less defined boys' adventure (at least in the sequential art format) forever after. With his erstwhile companions Captain Haddock ("Blistering barnacles!"), Professor Calculus, and the inspectors Thomson and Thompson, Tintin journeyed to practically every civilized and uncivilized nation in the world, through jungles and deserts, under the sea, and even into space. The very epitome of the can-do young adventurer, facing off against criminals, spies, and savages of every variety, this boy and his dog are incomparable guides for young men seeking vicarious exploration, action, and fun.

Compiled into three-story volumes or available in their original stand-alone editions, the stories are packed with mystery and thrills. They are bright, lively showpieces for the era in which they were produced (and the more "pure" sense of fun it offered), as well as excellent primers for the historical events of the time. By the same token, be aware that some of the depictions of minorities are also indicative of the era and the European sensibility that prevailed at the time.

Kim, Susan. *City of Spies*. First Second, 2010.

Genre: adventure
Discussion Topics: gender roles, life skills, politics, U.S. history, war, world history

Evelyn is sent to live with her Aunt Lia in the bohemian art world of 1942 New York. She longs for an absent family, but she has a potent fantasy life and finds a new friend in Tony, the superintendent's son. Together, always sniffing around for trouble, they stumble upon a real Nazi plot. The only problem is, who's going to believe them?

Pascal Dizin's uncanny ability to duplicate the sense of fantastic fun and adventure in Hergé's *Tintin* helps to escalate this exploit into something truly thrilling, but thanks to the strong writing, it also has a lot to say on just how much children still need to count on the adults in their lives.

Max Axiom, Super Scientist series. Capstone Press, 2007–.

Genre: nonfiction

Discussion Topics: racial/ethnic identity, science and technology

Max Axiom is a muscular African American scientist with a flowing white lab coat and reflective goggles. He may look like a superhero, but he provides excellent primers on all sorts of scientific disciplines, including electricity, magnetism, and sound; he also looks at more general issues such as the scientific method and global warming.

This series is not a replacement for a science text, but with its simple, precise explanations, glossaries, and "More About" sections, it's a good place for burgeoning scientists to start. GNs are an excellent way to get readers involved in subjects that might seem intimidating.

Sava, Scott Christian. *Cameron and His Dinosaurs*. IDW, 2009.

Genre: adventure

Discussion Topics: physically challenged

When a mad scientist creates four dinosaurs for the evil organization B.U.R.P.S., he's shocked to find that they have no interest in serving his nefarious plans. Instead, they come into the care of physically challenged eleven-year-old Cameron, who leads them in a rescue of the president of the United States.

Dinosaurs, adventure, and comedy are all great, but this also features practically the only wheelchair-bound hero (besides the X-Men's Professor X) in all comicdom.

Siegel, Siena Cherson. *To Dance: A Ballerina's Graphic Novel*. Atheneum, 2006.

Genre: biography

Discussion Topics: arts (dance), careers, gender roles, life skills

This book chronicles the journey of a young dancer, as Sienna dances on the beach as a child, is later inspired by the performance of a ballerina as a dying swan, and then pursues the rigorous discipline at Julliard.

The rare graphic novel that falls squarely within female interests, this book benefits from its most unusual subject matter. The narrator's love for the art of ballet comes through powerfully, thanks in great part to the warm, expressive art.

GRADES 5-7

Bio-Graphics series. ABDO, 2007–2009.

Genre: biography

Discussion Topics: gender roles, politics, prejudice, racial/ethnic identity, socioeconomic class, U.S. history, war

Sixteen titles provide a biographical overview of some of history's greatest social thinkers and reformers, from Sacagawea to Martin Luther King, Jr.

Solid historical bios cleverly include historical quotes within the narrative, as well as glossaries and lists for further reading. See www.abdopub.com/shop/pc/home.asp for a full list of titles; some standout choices include Anne Frank, Clara Barton, and Jackie Robinson.

*Butzer, C. M. *Gettysburg: The Graphic Novel*. HarperCollins, 2008.

Genre: nonfiction
Discussion Topics: politics, U.S. history, war

The most famous cemetery dedication in history is reproduced with a backdrop of art that depicts the ferocious battles and with the support of historical letters related to the subject.

Most students may have heard of the famous address, but the sentiments and reasoning behind it are likely obscure to them. Butzer brings home the emotion behind the history in a way that only sequential art can.

Davis, Eleanor. *The Secret Science Alliance and the Copycat Crook*. Bloomsbury USA, 2009.

Genre: adventure
Discussion Topics: gender roles, life skills, racial/ethnic identity, science and technology

Julian Calendar starts junior high at a new school and is tormented for appearing to be a science nerd. But when he finds a jock and a "troublemaker" who are as deeply committed to the pursuit of science as he is, the Secret Science Alliance is born. But can they stop an evil scientist from stealing their own ideas?

Davis's colorful, quality cartoon art highlights a smart story that not only understands the social difficulties of school popularity, but also blows stereotypes away and embraces intelligence and knowledge. The story includes schematics for some great, wild inventions, too.

DC Chronicles series. DC Comics, 2005–.

Genre: superhero
Discussion Topics: art history (comics), politics, U.S. history, war

DC Comics chronologically reprints the earliest Golden Age adventures of Superman, Wonder Woman, and Batman and the earliest Silver Age exploits of Flash and Green Lantern.

The Flash and Green Lantern books are wide-eyed, space-age adventures, and Wonder Woman is a fascinating glimpse into early female empowerment, but the Superman (by Jerry Siegel and Joe Shuster) and Batman (by Bill Finger and Bob Kane) books reprint the stories that actually created superheroes, and comics themselves, and are not to be missed. The art is rough-hewn and the action is straightforward, but the stories have simple narratives for the younger end and interesting takes on politics and justice (by no means unsophisticated) that will give older readers some food for thought. Great companion volumes for the Marvel Masterwork series included in this list.

Graphic Revolve Literary Classics series. Stone Arch Books, 2006–.

Genre: literary adaptation
Discussion Topics: art history (literature), U.S. history, world history

Like this imprint's mythology and fairy tale adaptations, these books capture the spirit and narrative events of the originals in an engaging form that feels fresh and lively. Obviously not intended to replace the works they adapt, these are a great way to pique interest or give a fresh perspective on a familiar story.

A full list of titles is available at www.stonearchbooks.com, but three titles that particularly reflect the atmosphere and interest of the originals are *The Hound of the Baskervilles* (by Martin Powell), *The Strange Case of Dr. Jekyll and Mr. Hyde* (by Carl Bowen), and *Alice in Wonderland* (by Martin Powell).

*Hale, Shannon. *Rapunzel's Revenge*. Bloomsbury USA, 2008. *Calamity Jack*. Bloomsbury USA, 2008.

Genre: adventure, fairy tale/folktale
Discussion Topics: coming-of-age, gender roles, life skills, U.S. history

In the Old West, spunky, self-reliant Rapunzel escapes from the tower, fights her evil mother, and discovers the secret of her own heritage with the help of her sidekick Jack. In the second adventure, Rapunzel joins Jack as he tries to leave his criminal past behind and gets tangled up with a giant beanstalk and a scheme to get the better of a wicked giant who has kidnapped his mother.

These fast-paced and extremely clever reimaginings of the fairytales put the action into a wonderfully weird historical setting, pull in a touch of steampunk, and put girl power right up front.

*Lee, Stan. Marvel Masterworks series. Marvel Comics, 1987–.

Genre: superhero
Discussion Topics: art history (comics), coming of age, family issues, life skills, politics, racial/ethnic identity, U.S. history, war

Reprints of the earliest adventures of Marvel's most popular superheroes, on glossy paper, are available in hardcover and paperback. (Marvel started the paperback program more recently, so fewer titles are available, but the selection grows every month.) The series has been produced for far longer than DC's Chronicles books, and the variety of heroes and time periods is much larger. As well, the sophistication of the storytelling is head and shoulders above other comics of this era, as Lee and his compatriots reimagined the superhero for new generations and redefined what the genre could be forever after. Mixing intelligent, emotional story lines with impressive and engaging characterizations and blazing action, weird and wonderful supervillains, snappy dialogue, dynamic art, and archetypes that will have real meaning to young readers, these are the superhero must-haves for your collection.

The range of heroes available in this series, from the family dynamic of the Fantastic Four to the antisocial antihero of the Hulk, truly offers something that will appeal to every reader of the age group (particularly boys). But, if you are going to get volumes focusing on only one character from the series (or if you are going with one superhero for your whole collection), then it should really be the *Amazing Spider-Man* volumes. Typifying the modern superhero with his mixture of personal angst, derring-do, and serious consideration of the role of personal responsibility, Spider-Man is the quintessential superhero of all time, and the power of the character is not lessened at all by the years since his inception. As a young adult superhero (long before the term *young adult* even existed) who spoke specifically to those concerns and fantasies, Spider-Man has the highest appeal to young readers with a taste for superheroes, and his adventures are the ones absolutely not to be missed.

O'Connor, George. Olympians series. First Second, 2010–.

Genre: mythology
Discussion Topics: art history (literature), family issues, world history

The mythological origins and adventures of Zeus, Athena, Hera, and Hades.

Though his mythology is meticulously researched and retold, O'Connor's graphic sensibility is pure Silver Age Marvel Comics, in the best way possible. This is creation myth as superhero origin, and the blazing, mountain-shattering battles rival the most spectacular movie blockbusters for sheer awe and spectacle.

*Phelan, Matt. *The Storm in the Barn.* Candlewick, 2009.

Genre: adventure
Discussion Topics: coming-of-age, family issues, illness, life skills, U.S. history

Eleven-year-old Jack lives in Dust Bowl, Kansas, in 1937, where there hasn't been a drop of rain in months. Hope grows short as Jack is tormented by the older boys, scorned by his father, and fears for his sister, who is wasting away in her bed. But in the neighbor's abandoned barn there is something lurking, something waiting to be discovered by a young boy with determination and nothing to lose.

Along with *The Arrival* (listed here), *The Storm in the Barn* is a contender for best GN ever produced. This is a coming-of-age story, a boy's adventure, a dark fantasy, a historical tale, and a loving homage to the power and art of storytelling itself. Wrapped in quiet, elegant, evocative art, Phelan's book captures the essence of a potent folktale and makes it live on the page.

Renier, Aaron. *Spiral Bound.* Top Shelf Productions, 2007.

Genre: adventure
Discussion Topics: gender roles, life skills

Burgeoning sculptor Turnip the elephant and his friends Stucky the dog and Ana the rabbit spend the summer honing their inventions and projects, but the mystery of the monster in the town woods take them on an unexpected adventure.

This satisfyingly weird adventure, in the vein of Roald Dahl, embraces a child's sense of invention and love of creative art with characters that, though they're animals, feel like real kids.

Sheinkin, Steve. Rabbi Harvey series. Jewish Lights, 2006–.

Genre: fairy tale/folktale, humor
Discussion Topics: life skills, religion, U.S. history

The most rootin'-tootin' tales ever told about a rabbi who takes the job of sheriff in an Old West frontier town. Harvey settles squabbles, protects the townfolk, and lives his life not by the speed of a quick draw, but with ancient wisdom and wry humor. All three volumes of this series (*The Adventures of Rabbi Harvey, Rabbi Harvey Rides Again,* and *Rabbi Harvey vs. the Wisdom Kid*) recount Harvey's life amidst the townfolk of Elk Spring, Colorado, in 1870, and all three are hilarious and filled with that most uncommon of treasures found anywhere in life: actual wisdom.

Combining a palette of washed-out Old West tones and distinctive, stylized art, with stories adapted from Jewish folklore and characters suffused with personality and sly humor (none more sweetly charismatic than the rabbi himself), Sheinkin has created something truly unique to the format. A joy for anyone who has a funny bone and is ready to learn something deeply true about life.

Sturm, James. *Satchel Paige: Striking Out Jim Crow*. Hyperion, 2007.

Genre: realistic fiction
Discussion Topics: family issues, prejudice, politics, racial/ethnic identity, socioeconomic class, U.S. history

In the rural South of 1944, a farmer and his son watch the legendary Paige, an iconic force against the Jim Crow laws, strike a blow for freedom on the baseball field.

Capturing the suspense of a great baseball game at the same time that it encapsulates the stark racism of the times, the story captures a moment in history that should never be forgotten.

Taylor, Sarah Stewart. *Amelia Earhart: This Broad Ocean*. Hyperion, 2010.

Genre: realistic fiction
Discussion Topics: careers, coming-of-age, gender roles, U.S. history, world history

When the famous aviatrix pauses in a history-making trip across the Atlantic at a small Newfoundland town for fuel, young "Nosy Nelly" is inspired by the female adventurer.

The Center for Cartoon Studies (which also published *Houdini: The Handcuff King* and *Satchel Paige: Striking Out Jim Crow,* both elsewhere on this list) has found a niche in portraying legendary figures in small snapshot moments of their lives and exploring how they affected the people of their times. This simple story touches on many themes, not just a young girl's inspiration, but also women's struggles to make headway in the professional world. The art, entirely white and blue, handily evokes the era, suggests a sense of lyrical grace, and washes the entire tale in the colors of the sky.

GRADES 6-8

Dembicki, Matt, ed. *Trickster: Native American Tales*. Fulcrum Publishing, 2010.

Genre: fairy tale/folktale
Discussion Topics: life skills, racial/ethnic identity, U.S. history

This collection of Native American folktales features the trickster archetype, produced by an array of creative talent in a variety of styles ranging from the humorous to the deeply affecting.

One of only a handful of GNs in existence that features Native American themes, this is also a great sampler of creative styles and showcases the potential of the form itself.

Dini, Paul. *World's Greatest Superheroes*. DC Comics, 2010.

Genre: superhero
Discussion Topics: politics, physically challenged, prejudice, socioeconomic class, terrorism, war

These superhero adventures address real-world issues and acknowledge that no super-powered savior is going to come along and actually fix these problems for us. Included are Superman (world hunger), Batman (crime), Wonder Woman (war, terrorism, and the role of diplomacy), and Captain Marvel (the plight of children, including physical disabilities, disease, and abuse). Also features a story with the Justice League of America as they battle a mysterious worldwide disease and an "Origins" section that covers both the famous and the obscure.

The partial picture book composition (the four main stories eschew word balloons and captions for more involved prose) and Alex Ross's astounding hyperrealistic painted art give these stories a sense of weight and reality appropriate to their more serious subject matter. These stories make great use of superheroes to both pay tribute to what is great about mankind and focus on what we still have to learn.

Homer. *The Odyssey*. Adapted by Tim Mucci. Sterling, 2010.

Genre: literary adaptation, mythology
Discussion Topics: art history (literature), family issues, politics, war, world history

Odysseus braves the dangers of one-eyed giants, sea creatures, sirens, and the underworld itself on his quest to get home.

While Odysseus's exploits are the basis for nearly all of modern adventure, from comics to summer blockbusters, *The Odyssey* tackles much deeper themes and motivations. Odysseus's quest is merely to get home to his family. His greatest challenges were not physical battles, but temptation. His greatest tool is his wits, and the greatest virtue of his day was faith in the gods and a sense of responsibility. The story is both a cracking good adventure and a glimpse into another era's philosophy. Ben Caldwell's art has a vibrant life that will make young readers feel like they're watching a *Samurai Jack* cartoon.

Kibuishi, Kazu. Amulet series. Graphix, 2008–.

Genre: adventure, fantasy
Discussion Topics: family issues, gender roles

After the shocking death of their father, siblings Emma and Navin move into an old family home with their mother. When she is lured through a magical door in the basement, the kids follow her through into an astonishing fantasyland of robots, demons, and talking animals. With the help of one of the local denizens, a mechanical rabbit, they rescue their mother . . . only to find her poisoned into a coma. Seeking help in the city of waterfalls only lands them in further trouble with the Elf King's son, and as they get caught up with other mysterious allies (or are they actually enemies?), the children seek to redeem the death of their father by saving their beloved mother.

Kibuishi's characters are well defined and possessed of accessible and identifiable traits. His fantasy environments and races are breathtakingly imagined, the situations thrilling, and the art delivered with a magical sheen that makes the tale seem almost animated. The father's death in a car accident at the beginning of the first book is not grisly but is gut-wrenchingly intense and sad (possibly too much so for some readers). This series delivers fantasy adventure and a powerful message.

Lee, Tony. *Outlaw: The Legend of Robin Hood*. Candlewick, 2009.

Genre: adventure, fairy tale/folktale
Discussion Topics: politics, religion, terrorism, world history

It's all here: Maid Marian, the sheriff of Nottingham, archery contests, duels, daring escapes, and romance.

The classic story wrapped in atmospheric shadows and a gritty tone—think Robin Hood by way of *Batman Begins* and *Casino Royale*. At the same time, the sense of Robin as a true hero in deed and philosophy is preserved for a generation of young male readers who might find a sense of rough heroism more palatable than its earnest antecedents. The same team produced a worthy follow-up in *Excalibur: The Legend of King Arthur*.

Lutes, Jason. *Houdini: The Handcuff King*. Hyperion, 2007.

Genre: biography
Discussion Topics: popular culture, U.S. history

A portrait of Houdini, the most famous man in the world at the time, as he makes preparations and then jumps into the freezing Boston River, while handcuffed, before an astonished crowd.

Over the course of a mere two-day narrative, readers gain a full and fascinating idea of Houdini's world, including introductions to those closest to him and the obsessions that drove him. The narrative captures the agonizing suspense surrounding Houdini's feat of escape, but also offers a salient commentary on the world of hype and celebrity. The book includes extensive and informative introduction and endnotes.

Ottaviani, Jim. *T-Minus: The Race to the Moon*. Aladdin, 2009.

Genre: realistic fiction
Discussion Topics: politics, science and technology, U.S. history, world history

From the earliest dreams of space travel through the race to the moon with the Russians, this is the story of the scientists, astronauts, and politics (on both sides of the world) that put man in space.

By focusing on the intellect of the scientists as much as the courage of astronauts and flyboys, Ottoviani tells a fascinating adventure of the mind and reminds us that even the most hard-core, practical science starts with a dream of imagination.

Sakai, Stan. Usagi Yojimbo series. Dark Horse, 1987–.

Genre: adventure
Discussion Topics: life skills, politics, war, world history

Closing in on thirty volumes of collected editions and still going strong, Sakai's venerable masterwork is the epic, ongoing tale of an honorable rabbit samurai in feudal Japan. Mixing an irresistible character who employs his intelligence and compassion as often as his (highly skilled) sword arm, these terrific adventures combine accurate historical details, legends from Japanese folklore, and samurai action to tell a story of honor and intrigue that has, by benefit of its vast run, achieved a depth and complexity seldom found in GNs.

Sakai's deceptively simple cartoon animals serve as the perfect counterpoint to the exhaustively researched historical and folkloric details included in every story (with an author's explanation and notes at the end), as well as the complex narrative threads and elements of intrigue and supporting characters that wind through multiple volumes. It's easy enough to leap in anywhere, though reading from beginning to end is a remarkably involving (and time-consuming) experience. If you're hesitant to commit to the whole thing, a few volumes that work well on their own are *Volume 1: Ronin, Volume 12: Grasscutter, Volume 23: Bridge of Tears,* and *Usagi Yojimbo: Yokai* (the first Usagi Yojimbo story in color).

Smith, Jeff. Bone series. Cartoon Books, 1991–2004.

Genre: adventure, fantasy
Discussion Topics: gender roles, life skills, politics, war

The trials and tribulations of the three Bone cousins and the princess-in-hiding, Thorn, as they cross a vast fantasy landscape in their heroes' journey to save the world.

Told in nine collected volumes, Smith's epic adventure fantasy is part *Lord of the Rings* and part *Uncle Scrooge* and was one of the very early GN titles to gain shelf space in libraries. With the well-balanced mix of comedy and adventure, emotional range and epic sweep, it's not hard to see why. Smith's art has a deceptively simple line and a gentle charm, while the storytelling has both a captivating surface energy and a deeper level of emotional and social complexity. Although the volumes can be read individually, the ideal way to experience the full grandeur is from beginning to end (assorted specials that feature some characters in stand-alone stories are nice add-ons, but not necessary). One of the true classics of the field.

*Tan, Shaun. *The Arrival*. Arthur A. Levine Books, 2007.

Genre: fantasy
Discussion Topics: arts (visual), family issues, language arts, life skills, politics, prejudice, racial/ethnic identity, socioeconomic class, U.S. history, war, world history

A man leaves his family and his home and seeks his fortune in a new land. Once there, he must navigate a vast, unfamiliar city crowded with words, ways, and people he can't understand. Slowly, with the friendship of fellow immigrants who each have harrowing tales of their own journeys, he begins to make a new life for himself, in hopes of bringing his family to join him.

From this simple, universal tale of a stranger in a strange land, Tan creates a work of art actually unparalleled in the medium. One of the few works of sequential art that could rightfully be considered graphic literature and, quite possibly, the greatest GN of all time, *The Arrival* actually expands the potential of the medium on every page and uses the form as never before. Everything from panel sequencing, image textures, and evolving palette deepen the emotional resonance of this completely silent tale (the only words are written in an invented language to highlight the immigrant's isolation). The visual metaphors at once are simple enough for young readers to follow and also convey a lifetime's worth of emotional potency, and the simple imaginative flourishes (the complicated commerce of the new land, a manga-inspired animal that befriends the man) create incredible personal investment. A resounding achievement for the form, as both art and social commentary.

Telgemeier, Raina. *Smile.* **Graphix, 2010.**

Genre: biography
Discussion Topics: coming-of-age, family issues, gender roles, life skills, sexuality

After an accident knocks her two front teeth out as a child, Raina grows up dealing with a whirlwind of dental surgery and self-image issues, which in the end help her find strength to go her own way.

This coming-of-age story uses the unusual element of dental problems to highlight its classic issues of confidence and self-image. Emotional issues of family and the question of friends who might not have your best interest at heart are skillfully and subtly woven into the narrative.

Vollmar, Rob. *The Castaways.* **ComicsLit, 2008.**

Genre: realistic fiction
Discussion Topics: coming-of-age, family issues, prejudice, racial/ethnic identity, socioeconomic class, U.S. history

During the Great Depression, thirteen-year-old Tucker is forced to leave home and ends up hopping trains. Under the tutelage of an old African American hobo, Tucker learns the ins and outs of an itinerant life and a society of the disenfranchised that lives just outside the world we see.

Drawing from our collective American mythology, Vollmar captures the desperation of the era and the need to live by a code regardless of what community you belong to. At the same time, he creates a tale that resonates with melancholy and a deep longing for a home.

7
Annotated Reading Lists
GRADES 9 THROUGH 12

IT WILL COME AS NO SURPRISE THAT THE TITLES IN THIS chapter move into more mature territory. Several discussion topics appear here for the first time, and several that appeared in chapter 6 now indicate a more sophisticated approach. Life skills, for instance, are much different for a fifteen-year-old than for an eight-year-old. The specifics should be quite clear in the annotations. For a list of titles by discussion topic, please consult the index of discussion topics.

You will find the realistic fiction genre combining with some unexpected partners such as the superhero and science fiction genres. This indicates that a central device (someone with superpowers, for instance) is put in a narrative whose elements, tone, and themes reflect intensely realistic situations and social issues.

The division between recommendations for grade levels 9–10 and grade levels 11–12 is blurry, and many of the titles work across the board. The recommendations that follow are based for the most part on the complexity with which the themes are handled rather than on the themes themselves.

GRADES 9-10

Abadzis, Nick. *Laika.* First Second, 2007.

Genre: realistic fiction
Discussion Topics: politics, science and technology, world history

The story of the Russian space program as seen through the eyes of the dog Laika, the first living creature to exit Earth's atmosphere; Yelena, a lab technician who developed a deep attachment to the canine; and Korolev, once a political prisoner but now the program's top engineer.

A spiritual companion for Ottaviani's *T-Minus: The Race to the Moon* (listed in the previous chapter), this book mixes paranoia-inducing politics and frontier-blazing science with intense emotion. Yelena's trials and feelings for Laika put the humanity into the history and help open up the culture of Soviet Russia itself. But be warned: Laika's destiny was a glorious one, but it also doomed him to a premature death.

*Bendis, Brian Michael. Ultimate Spider-Man series. Marvel Comics, 2000–.

Genre: superhero
Discussion Topics: coming-of-age, dating and relationships, gender roles, family issues, life skills

High school outcast Peter Parker gets bitten by the radioactive spider, learns the hard lesson of power and responsibility, and grows up contending not only with supervillains, but also with the emotional rigors of girlfriends, friendships, and family.

A contemporary retelling of the mythology, this is the quintessential modern superhero comic, featuring the quintessential everyman hero. The stories, in homage to their predecessors, display a high degree of emotional complexity as Peter negotiates terrain familiar to any teenager. The series is available in many collected forms, and although the characters continue, the story arcs are fairly self-enclosed, so each is a fine jumping-on point. If your selection is limited, try to pick up a collection containing the story "Confessions," originally featured in *Ultimate Spider-Man* 13 (generally included in volume 2 of most collections—but not always). This actionless tale takes place completely within Peter Parker's room, exploring trust and young relationships as he reveals to girlfriend Mary Jane the truth of his secret identity.

Bilson, Danny. *Red Menace*. Wildstorm, 2007.

Genre: superhero
Discussion Topics: politics, U.S. history

The Eagle is a crime fighter in the 1950s, a patriotic ex-soldier who takes on criminals with two fists and a roaring .45. But when red-baiting politicians decide he's their next target, he must team up with a young, superpowered amateur to clear his name.

A standard superhero adventure takes on extra weight with this historical lesson that drives home the point that in the culture of paranoia and mistrust in 1950s America, anyone could end up under suspicion. Jerry Ordway's clean, detailed, and realistic art is ideal for its classical evocation of the time and its expert sense of movement.

Bradbury, Ray. *Ray Bradbury's Fahrenheit 451*. Adapted by Tim Hamilton. Hill and Wang, 2009.

Genre: literary adaptation
Discussion Topics: art history (literature), dating and relationships, family issues, politics

An author-approved adaptation of the Bradbury's classic about fireman Guy Montag, who is charged with the job of burning books, dangerous objects in a society of numb, government-conditioned people. But when Montag is brought into the confidence of a young woman, he begins to see the injustice of authority and the value of free thought.

The atmospheric art is drenched in shadows that highlight the oppression of Montag's world. Bradbury's statement is timeless and incredibly important, and this GN is an excellent way for young adults to discover it or to supplement their understanding of the book.

Busiek, Kurt. Astro City series. Wildstorm, 1999–.

Genre: superhero
Discussion Topics: dating and relationships, family issues, gender roles, life skills, prejudice, racial/ethnic identity

Welcome to Astro City, where the human characters, effects, and consequences come before the superpowers.

Busiek and Anderson have built an entire universe with all the great superheroic types represented and use it as a springboard to tell deeply moving stories about normal people in extraordinary situations. The series combines the best of both the world-building mythology that fans crave with the stand-alone, insightful storytelling that appeals to fresh readers. Every collection has much to recommend it, but if you're going for only one, get *Volume 2: Confession*. The main story turns a coming-of-age theme into the best sidekick story ever (and features vampires, no less), but you can get this one solely on the basis of the short backup story "The Nearness of You," as fine a story of love and longing as has ever been written in any medium.

Campbell, Ross. *Shadow Eyes*. SLG Publishing, 2010.

Genre: adventure, science fiction
Discussion Topics: dating and relationships, family issues, gender roles, life skills, racial/ethnic identity, sexual orientation, socioeconomic class

In the dystopian future city of Dranac, a teenage African American girl mutates into a weird blue creature and becomes a superhero, running away from home and rescuing a lost girl from a zombie.

Yes, the plot sounds unrealistic, but Campbell's writing offers layered characters, emotional situations, complex friendships and relationships, and the most realistic teen dialogue I've ever read in any form. It is also a great step toward diversifying the format, with a cast of strong female, African American characters and the GN form's lone (as far as I know) transsexual character (who is handled with taste and without histrionics). Far-out trappings, but a world and language teens will be very familiar with and comfortable diving into.

Canada, Geoffrey. *Fist Stick Knife Gun: A Personal History of Violence*. Adapted by Jamar Nicholas. Beacon Press, 2010.

Genre: biography
Discussion Topics: coming-of-age, life skills, politics, prejudice, racial/ethnic identity, socioeconomic class, U.S. history

Drawing upon Canada's book, Nicholas recounts life growing up on the streets of the South Bronx during the 1960s and 1970s, where you had to learn to navigate your way around—and often through—an ever-expanding terrain of violence. Such a life required quick reflexes plus subtle understanding of the politics and dynamics that violence creates.

Not a call to abolish violence, but a much more realistic recognition that it is necessary to take control of the violence that is inevitable and unavoidable in so many lives. Canada's authentic voice hammers home the fact that a cool head is far more important than a fist, a stick, a knife, or a gun.

Carey, Mike. *Ender's Game: Battle School.* Christopher Yost. *Ender's Shadow: Battle School.* Marvel Comics, 2009.

Genre: science fiction
Discussion Topics: family issues, life skills, politics, religion, war

Each GN adapts the opening section of Orson Scott Card's sci-fi classics. *Ender's Game* is about the brilliant Ender Wiggin, swept away from his family to attend the rigorous Battle School, where young children are trained to become a defense against an imminent alien invasion. For Ender the school is not just a place to learn strategy, but also a battleground where he must face the dark forces of his own psyche. *Ender's Shadow* tells the parallel tale of Bean, Ender's equally intelligent lieutenant, who is recruited for the school from the deadly streets where he has been orphaned. For him, the school is a struggle with a manipulative authority and a place to begin the quest for answers about his own past.

Card's original Ender book is a well-deserved classic, touching on a number of large themes and situating them in a teen-familiar environment with accessible personal issues. The adaptations carry all the strengths into a graphic format and function exceptionally well together, as Ender's and Bean's journeys play out similar struggles from different perspectives, highlighting the emotional issues with a depth that most single narratives can't generally manage.

Carey, Mike. *Re-Gifters.* Minx, 2007.

Genre: realistic fiction
Discussion Topics: careers, coming-of-age, dating and relationships, gender roles, life skills

Dixie is a Korean American teen gearing up for the big hapkido competition. But when she develops a crush on a fellow martial arts student, her focus and her friendships suffer. The trick now is winning her way back into the tournament and finding the best part of herself again.

An energetic, upbeat, girl-powered story with real emotion underscoring the fun.

Castellucci, Cecil. *The Plain Janes.* Minx, 2007.

Genre: realistic fiction
Discussion Topics: coming-of-age, family issues, gender roles, life skills, terrorism

Whisked away from the big city after a traumatic incident, Jane is determined not to be driven into seclusion by her fears. She rallies a small group of fellow outcasts into a band of "art terrorists," creating simultaneous works of art and civil disobedience in an attempt to shake their conservative community out of its malaise.

This book is a great example of girl power in GNs, with appealing—and appealingly flawed—characters and a significant, teen-relevant message about idealism and obeying the rules. A sequel, *Plain Janes in Love,* continues the scoring with a focus on relationships.

Cavallaro, Michael. *Parade (with Fireworks)*. Image Comics, 2009.

Genre: realistic fiction
Discussion Topics: family issues, politics, war, world history

In 1920s Italy, the life of a young man is changed forever when an argument between the socialists and the fascists in his small town breaks out into deadly violence.

Distinctive art that is both evocative of the classical setting but modern in its style will draw teens into this tale of battling political ideologies and underscore the impact that one person's beliefs can have on an entire community.

Cooke, Darwyn. *DC: The New Frontier* (volumes 1 and 2 or the Absolute Edition). DC Comics, 2004–2006.

Genre: superhero
Discussion Topics: gender roles, prejudice, racial/ethnic identity, U.S. history, war

A huge cast of superheroes confronts the political problems (McCarthyism, prejudice, war) and scientific advances (space travel) that America faced as the Cold War kicked into high gear, even as an insidious, powerful alien force begins to emerge.

A sprawling superhero epic that honors the transition of the Golden Age of comics to the Silver Age, even as it gives incisive examination to the political forces at work during America's turbulent space age. Characters such as Superman, Batman, and Wonder Woman are cast in smaller roles that underscore particular political issues, as the spotlight falls on characters such as Green Lantern (a test pilot) and the Flash (a scientist) who have much more personal dilemmas that flesh out the ethical concerns and wonders of scientific advancement that the average man was contending with at the time. Cooke's extraordinary blending of art deco design and robust character work has a unique aesthetic in contemporary comic art.

Dunning, John Harris. *Salem Brownstone*. Candlewick, 2010.

Genre: fantasy
Discussion Topics: arts (visual)

Young magician Salem Brownstone inherits a magical orb from his late father, but it is coveted by the Seven Dark Elders of Midnight City. Only with the aid of Dr. Kinoshita's Circus, and a very dry wit, can Salem survive.

Never has a plot summary been so inadequate in transmitting the value and power of a book. From its purple bound cover to its psychedelic black-and-white illustration, this book is in every sense a work of art. The two first-time creators (Nikhil Singh is the artist) have made something unique in the field, with haunting images that will stay with readers for a lifetime and an abiding sense of strangeness that seems to touch something metaphysical. This is the book to hand to the quiet outcast and to discuss in every art class from eighth grade up.

Geary, Rick. *The Murder of Abraham Lincoln*. ComicsLit, 2005.

Genre: nonfiction
Discussion Topics: politics, U.S. history

Billed as "a chronicle of 62 days in the life of the American Republic—March 4th–May 4th, 1865," Geary's work traces the assassination starting with Lincoln's second oath of office, through the planning of Booth and his compatriots, to the deed itself and its immediate aftermath. The book follows the route of Lincoln's funeral train as it tours the country and describes the pursuit of Booth as he is burned alive in a surrounded barn, refusing to surrender.

This book is the jewel in the crown of Geary's eminently worthwhile Treasury of Victorian Murder series. Every aspect of the historical event is examined and meticulously researched. The inclusion of historical facts and well-supported suppositions about the president's condition and state of mind do not detract one iota from the suspense of watching the history-shaking event play out. A bibliography and three maps of pertinent areas are evidence that Geary is the world's premiere graphic historian.

Gipi. *Notes for a War Story*. First Second, 2007.

Genre: war and consequences
Discussion Topics: coming-of-age, life skills, socioeconomic class, war, world history

In a nameless Balkan war zone, three aimless friends fall in with a dangerous war profiteer, ending up in his employ, where their youth, greed, and class jealousy lead them down a dark road.

A grim book that doesn't pull punches about how little choice, how little hope there is when your entire world is surrounded by war and those who seek to profit by the misfortune of others. The teens are portrayed with great realism, and only one seems to have even a chance at a promising future. Disturbing but realistic and accessible.

Gonick, Larry. Cartoon History series. Doubleday, 1991–.

Genre: nonfiction
Discussion Topics: politics, science and technology, U.S. history, war, world history

Gonick has created an amazingly thorough array of history books that cover the United States, the modern world, and the universe itself. Each history contains multiple volumes with indexes, and each is packed with information laid out in a complete but unintimidating fashion, taking full advantage of the humorous possibilities of the form.

Gonick starts the U.S. history with Columbus, the modern world with the U.S. Constitution, and the universe with—what else?—the Big Bang. Each history provides a well-thought-out and clearly explained overview that can serve as an effective supplement to textbooks, offering the overall sweep of history in an engaging way, while the textbook focuses on the detailed facts. Gonick has expanded his cartoon guides into other areas, too, including genetics, computers, statistics, physics, the environment, and sex.

Hinds, Gareth. *Beowulf*. Candlewick, 2007.

Genre: mythology
Discussion Topics: family issues, world history

A graphic and prose retelling of the epic poem, centering on the fierce warrior Beowulf, who tore the arm from the monstrous and blood-thirsty Grendel and then confronted the creature's wily and powerful mother.

A 1,200-year-old poem viewed as video game action extravaganza, this is nowhere near as pandering as it could have been. The battles are intensely choreographed (particularly the aquatic showdown at the end) and the atmosphere is thick with cavernous halls and shadowy caves, but the tone of the original is absolutely given its due, and the obsession with legacies between fathers and sons is carried over with great weight.

Hine, David. Spider-Man Noir series. Marvel Comics, 2009.

Genre: superhero
Discussion Topics: drug use, life skills, sexuality, socioeconomic class, U.S. history

The Spider-Man legend is reimagined in a dark, Depression-era New York City, with all the familiar supporting players and villains cast in new roles.

Turning Spider-Man into a pulp figure gives the familiar character a new spin (so to speak), but the writing also uses period-specific details such as prohibition, corruption, and the role of the press to make deeper points. Peter Parker's journey and responsibility are also given a new weight, as he starts off seeking revenge but comes to understand that there's more to being a hero.

Johns, Geoff. *Green Lantern: Secret Origin.* DC Comics, 2009.

Genre: superhero
Discussion Topics: coming-of-age, life skills

Ace test pilot Hal Jordan is inducted into the Green Lantern Corps, an interstellar law enforcement army. But before he can start making war on the bad guys, he must first master the most powerful weapon in the universe, a ring that can create anything he can imagine, powered by his own willpower. His teacher: Sinestro, a man with little patience and a dark destiny of his own.

Johns rebuilds Green Lantern's origin and mythology for newcomers and fans alike, giving Hal Jordan a believably hotshot personality that teen boys won't be able to resist and putting him into a high-tension teacher-student relationship.

Johnson, Mat. *Incognegro.* Vertigo, 2009.

Genre: realistic fiction
Discussion Topics: prejudice, racial/ethnic identity, U.S. history

Zen Pinchback is a light-skinned African American reporter in 1930s New York who makes his living going "incognegro," posing as a white man and infiltrating hate groups in the South. Now Zane must investigate the arrest of his own brother, charged with the savage murder of a white woman.

A fascinating piece of little-known history is explored in a story that is both a mystery and a deft examination of the time and culture in which prejudice thrived most virulently.

Kirkman, Robert. Invincible series. Image Comics, 2003–.

Genre: superhero
Discussion Topics: coming-of-age, dating and relationships, family issues, life skills

Teenager Mark Grayson has inherited the superpowers of his father, Omni-Man, a superhero of extraterrestrial origin. Over the course of the series Mark faces the difficulty of fitting in with other superheroes, a stunning betrayal by his father, and every imaginable trial Kirkman can stuff into his epic modernization of the teen superhero.

Taking the premise of Spider-Man (a teen character who must contend with both adolescent life and superpowered tribulations) to an extreme degree, Kirkman has put the metaphor into a highly accessible, contemporary story that confronts teen issues realistically and incites heavy emotional investment with some shocking plot twists. Particular weight is given to exploring the dynamics of father-son relationships.

Kurtzman, Harvey. EC Archives: Two-Fisted Tales series. Dark Horse, 2007.

Genre: war and consequences
Discussion Topics: art history (comics), politics, prejudice, U.S. history, war, world history

Though they were written in the 1950s—one of the titles was in fact responsible for the development of the Comics Code Authority—these are still the sharpest, most emotionally resonant tales comics have ever told about war. While the first few issues feature a smattering of battles in other eras (pirates, Greeks, cowboys), the title quickly began focusing its anthology of tales on World War II, using it as a backdrop for social commentary, sharp political criticism, and shockingly insightful (and often disturbing) considerations of what war can do to a human soul.

The soon-to-be legendary artists who contributed work gave each story a distinctive style and, for an American comic in the 1950s, the writing had a remarkably balanced perspective on the so-called enemy. If you're getting only a single volume, go for the second, as it features the story "Corpse on the Imjin," which is among the most powerful statements on the conditions of the fighting man and the toll battle can take available in any medium.

Larson, Hope. *Chiggers*. Aladdin, 2008.

Genre: realistic fiction
Discussion Topics: coming-of-age, dating and relationships, gender roles, life skills

Abby's latest visit to summer camp finds her relationships with her friends changing as she finds herself getting close to a strange and unpopular girl named Shasta. At the same time, she struggles through awkwardness to get to know a boy named Teal. The drama is ultimately given form in a climax that uses a gentle dose of magical realism that heightens its emotional power.

Larson does a masterful job of capturing the political dynamic of teen girls' relationships and the nervous and wonderful feeling of young romance, even as she underscores that melancholy of letting go of childhood.

*Loeb, Jeph. *Superman for All Seasons*. DC Comics, 2002.

Genre: superhero
Discussion Topics: careers, coming-of-age, family issues, gender roles, life skills

Superman's early life and first steps as a superhero told over four seasons, each by a different narrator. Through the words of Pa Kent, Lois Lane, Lex Luthor, and Superman himself we see Superman's early days in Smallville; his arrival in Metropolis, where he must establish himself not only as a hero, but also as a reporter for the *Daily Planet;* and his first meetings with his greatest love and his greatest enemy.

Never before (or since) has the superhero concept been so well cast as American mythology. All the story beats feel fresh and alive at the same time that they are familiar and archetypal, pulled from a place in the great American cultural consciousness that few fictional characters inhabit as well as Superman. It's all the more effective because Clark Kent is portrayed not just as a staunch defender of truth and justice, but primarily as a young man, away from his parents and his home for the first time, fitting into a new world, and trying to make it a better place even as he begins to understand who he can be.

Mathieu, Marc-Antoine. *Museum Vaults: Excerpts from the Journal of an Expert.* **ComicsLit, 2008.**

Genre: fantasy
Discussion Topics: art history (visual)

In this dark French import, a museum inspector and his assistant go on a surreal, decades-long journey that plumbs the depth of a museum loosely based on France's Louvre. As they descend deeper and deeper, encountering museum workers and pieces of historically significant (and real) art, the purpose of their quest becomes more and more obscure.

Mathieu's book is a uniquely French blend of art history, philosophy, and existential surrealism. The tone and the stark black-and-white art, drenched in shadow, are unlike anything available from American publishers.

*McCloud, Scott. *Understanding Comics.* **Harper, 1994.**

Genre: nonfiction
Discussion Topics: art history (comics), arts (visual)

Creator and artist McCloud guides readers through every step of the process, from how stories are created to how and why we perceive them in a particular way, and he does it all in sequential art form. Two further volumes, *Making Comics* and *Reinventing Comics,* expound on the process and future of comic production, also in comic form.

This seminal work in analyzing the form is made as charming and engaging as it can be, given McCloud's panache with the form. It's great not just for comic readers, but also for anyone interested in the arts and how human beings express themselves.

McCreery, Connor. *Kill Shakespeare, Volume 1.* **IDW, 2010.**

Genre: fantasy, literary adaptation
Discussion Topics: art history (literature), family issues, politics

In cahoots with Lady Macbeth, the tyrant Richard III manipulates the anguished Hamlet into seeking out the mysterious wizard, William Shakespeare, to steal his quill. Accompanied by Richard's man Iago, Hamlet is soon whisked away by Falstaff and joins up with a rebellion against the king, led by Othello and Juliet Montague.

An exceedingly clever device actually fulfills its potential by faithfully interpreting and fleshing out Shakespeare's characters (particularly the manipulative Iago and the rascally Falstaff) and by creating a number of scenes and situations that read true to the plays and follow through on many of Shakespeare's themes. The art envisions the characters and many of the environments with a most appropriate theatricality.

McKeever, Sean. Spider-Man Loves Mary Jane series. Marvel Comics, 2005–.

Genre: realistic fiction, superhero
Discussion Topics: coming-of-age, dating and relationships, gender roles, life skills

The complicated romance between the teen superhero and his heartthrob is familiar from the movies, but this charming series tells the tale from Mary Jane's perspective.

This superhero tale isn't a male power fantasy, but actually a sweet, smart tale of high school drama featuring a charming and identifiable heroine who faces real-life, age-appropriate trials. Think of it as an updated *Archie* that's serious, but not too serious. No previous knowledge of the situation is necessary because the series builds its own effective continuity, but Moore's first volume, called *Sophomore Jinx,* provides a convenient starting point for newcomers.

*Millar, Mark. *Civil War*. Marvel Comics, 2008.

Genre: superhero, war and consequences
Discussion Topics: life skills, politics

After a group of irresponsible superheroes accidentally destroys a small town, the government responds with the Superhero Registration Act: all superheroes must reveal their secret identities and take assignments from government authorities. A number of heroes capitulate, seeing the reason for this development. Other heroes believe that doing this will make them pawns of government powers, bereft of free choice. And you know what happens when superheroes disagree, right? Big fights.

Along with *Captain America: The Chosen* (also on this list), this is the best example of the superhero genre offering incisive social commentary on contemporary issues. Interspersed with the punches and explosions, significant issues of security versus privacy are raised and debated with weight and intellectual consideration. As a major event within the Marvel Comics universe, *Civil War* served as a central book with many other comics deepening and expanding the narrative. Of the twenty-plus titles available, the two to pick up (though you don't need anything beyond the main book) are *Civil War: Spider-Man,* featuring the hero's struggle with revealing his identity and the drama of realizing he's chosen the wrong side, and *Civil War: New Avengers,* featuring a story with Luke Cage (an African American superhero) that is an excellent depiction of a man who wants only peace being forced into a corner for the sake of a principle.

*Morales, Robert. *Captain America: Truth*. Marvel Comics, 2004.

Genre: realistic fiction, superhero
Discussion Topics: politics, prejudice, racial/ethnic identity, U.S. history, war

Comic book lore has many interpretations of how weak and scrawny but brave and committed Steve Rogers was given the supersoldier formula and transformed into Captain America, living legend of World War II. *Truth* posits (with disturbing historical precedence) that the serum was first tested on African American soldiers to an array of effects ranging from the catastrophic to the successful. Isaiah Bradley, one of the guinea pigs that the formula transformed into a powerful specimen, becomes the first Captain America, a hero his nation never knew of who, despite his service, faded into history . . . until now.

Using appalling historical events like the syphilis experiments conducted on impoverished African Americans at Tuskegee University, Morales and Baker explore a very dark corner in the history of a very bright hero. Bradley is a powerfully realized character, an American soldier with a deep commitment to his country but who, like many men and women throughout history, was misused and then disowned by that country.

Neri, G. *Yummy: The Last Days of a Southside Shorty.* **Lee and Low, 2010.**

Genre: biography
Discussion Topics: family issues, racial/ethnic identity, socioeconomic class

The true story of Robert Sandifer, who was a hardened gang member, a thief, a killer, and a dead body all by the age of eleven. Narrated by a fictionalized classmate who is scared straight by "Yummy's" tragic tale, this is a tightly researched account of an inescapable sociopolitical truth.

That extreme poverty can lead young people into lives of crime and violence is a tale so often told that it can become numbing. Neri's narrative brings the message home in a personal way, aided by Randy DuBurke's gritty black-and-white art, returning a much needed urgency to the message.

Novgorodoff, Danica. *Refresh, Refresh.* **First Second, 2009.**

Genre: realistic fiction, war and consequences
Discussion Topics: coming-of-age, family issues, life skills, socioeconomic class, war

Their fathers fighting in Iraq, three boys are stuck in a nowhere town, filled with fear for their families and facing responsibilities they don't want. Trapped between boyhood and manhood, they seem to have no choices open to them except bad ones.

The war and the absence of the fathers haunt this story from beginning to end, painting a disturbing portrait of children who are afforded neither fair time to grow up nor the role models they so desperately need.

Pyle, Kevin C. *Katman.* **Henry Holt, 2009.**

Genre: realistic fiction
Discussion Topics: coming-of-age, dating and relationships, gender roles, life skills, socioeconomic class

Kit, his single mother, and his angry brother are all stuck in low-income housing with dim prospects. Derided by his peers, Kit finds a direction and strength to stand up for himself by becoming the custodian of the neighborhood's stray cats.

A parable for accepting responsibility and opening yourself up to relationships and possibilities, the story also has the valuable quality of turning stereotypes on their heads and offers a fresh look at classic ideas.

Runberg, Sylvain. *Orbital, Volume 1: Scars and Volume 2: Ruptures.* **Cinebooks, 2009.**

Genre: adventure, science fiction
Discussion Topics: gender roles, politics, prejudice

A human teams up with an alien to promote peace on behalf of an interstellar coalition that despises him.

The atypical art (for American comics anyway) in this European import creates distinctive visual personalities and a murky atmosphere for both the environments and politics. This is classic science fiction at its best, a story of ideas and a commentary on who we are, cloaked in an adventure about who we're going to be.

Schrag, Ariel, ed. *Stuck in the Middle: Seventeen Comics from an Unpleasant Age.* **Viking, 2007.**

Genre: humor, realistic fiction
Discussion Topics: dating and relationships, family issues, gender roles, life skills, sexuality

Seventeen indie-comic artists revisit their (older) middle school days from an adult perspective, though one that is clearly still affected by the various travails of the time. As the storytellers here all grew up to be comic creators, a classically (or at least stereotypically) geeky group, they shared the experience of being an outcast to greater or lesser degrees. But few who have ever been in a school haven't felt that at some point or another, and there is something here for everyone who has ever felt awkward and uncomfortable.

All the big issues are tackled: family, friendship, envy, dating, heartbreak, acne, and going to the bathroom (in perhaps the most squirm-inducing but also most painfully accessible of the stories). The discomfort here is quite palpable and should find a devoted following in high school students who are just coming out of or still going through these issues, and who will be relieved to see that some pains are truly universal. Creators include Daniel Clowes (*Ghost World*) and Aaron Renier (*Spiral Bound*), among many other talented, if lesser-known, artists.

Sfar, Joann. Dungeon series. Nantier Beall Minoustchine Publishing, 2004–.

Genre: fantasy, humor
Discussion Topics: politics, war

An import from French comics superstar Sfar, *Dungeon* is a hilarious parody of sword-and-sorcery adventure. Inhabited by funny animal characters, it nominally focuses on Herbert the Duck, whose family is in charge of the Dungeon itself, a vast complex where monsters lurk and treasure awaits—a sort of medieval amusement park for adventurers.

Actually several series in one, the entire history of the Dungeon is related from past (in *Dungeon: Early Years*) to future (in *Dungeon: Twilight,* the darkest of the various series), but if you're only going for one, *Dungeon: Zenith,* recounting the place's "present" adventures, is rock solid fun. The mixture of lowbrow and highbrow humor leaves no single fantasy cliché unassaulted.

*Shakespeare, William. Classical Comics adaptations. Classical Comics, 2008–.

Genre: literary adaptation
Discussion Topics: art history (literature), world history

Classical Comics has developed a fascinating system geared specifically to curricular use. Each work is adapted into three forms (all with the same art): original text, which features Shakespeare's unabridged words; plain text, which translates the play into modern English but retains the density of the words; and quick text, which translates the language into a fast, simplified version that still manages to convey the drama and theme.

The danger here, of course, is that students will opt to read only the quick text and lose out on much of what makes Shakespeare's work so rich and powerful. However, using two versions in tandem for a unit or lesson is an excellent opportunity to explore the various levels on which Shakespeare told his tales. The best of Classical Comics' offerings in its

Shakespeare line is, hands down, *The Tempest* (by John McDonald and John Haward), with its vibrant color palette and full use of the form's strength and potential to make the Bard's most fantastical work feel truly magical.

Shakespeare, William. Manga Shakespeare series. Abrams, 2007–.

Genre: literary adaptation
Discussion Topics: art history (literature), world history

Using alternate settings, the heaviest abridgements, and the fastest, most recognizable form, these adaptations are likely to be the most popular with the average student. They all have serviceable art, capture the tone and thrust of the plays, and are surely the best for students most resistant to investigating Shakespeare. One that stands out is the raw and striking *Julius Caesar* (by Mustashrik). It uses spare but intense art to capture the characters' internal lives and does a potent job of visualizing the Bard's tale of assassination, revenge, and conscience, especially in the depiction of Caesar's assassination itself, which, through gripping use of shadow, is made both subtle and graphic at the same time.

Siddell, Thomas. Gunnerkrigg Court series. Archaia Studios Press, 2009–.

Genre: adventure, fantasy
Discussion Topics: life skills

Antimony knows nothing about the weird boarding school she's just been sent to. With her best friend, her guardian demon (in the form of a dog), and her robot, she goes about plumbing its mysteries as well as the secret of what lurks beyond its walls.

Taken from Siddell's webcomic, this reads like Harry Potter with a female protagonist and a deep, eerie sense of the weird. The industrial design of the environments and the manga styling of the characters combine for a unique look, and the slow unraveling of the many mysteries makes for a very compelling read.

Simone, Gail. *Wonder Woman: The Circle*. DC Comics, 2009.

Genre: superhero
Discussion Topics: dating and relationships, gender roles, politics, war

A menace from Wonder Woman's earliest history seeks revenge as the Amazon establishes herself in "man's world" and returns to her abandoned home to confront her past.

Wonder Woman has long been portrayed (by predominantly male writers) as a male hero who happens to be female. But for the first time, Wonder Woman has a distinct and believable character that offers some insight into the differences in the way men and women handle situations. Also, an unusual plea for peaceful solutions and a morally complex array of "villains"—both in the main story and the backup—make for an exceptional read that invites thoughtful consideration.

Sinclair, Upton. *The Jungle*. Adapted by Peter Kuper. Papercutz, 2010.

Genre: literary adaptation
Discussion Topics: art history (literature), careers, family issues, life skills, politics, prejudice, sexuality, socioeconomic class, U.S. history

Sinclair's influential 1906 novel (it was the impetus for reforming the meat-packing industry) tells of immigrant Jurgis Rudkus, who wants nothing more than a stable life for himself and his family in America. But with every step, every turn, he runs afoul of bad fortune and corruption until he has nothing left but the guttering flame of hope.

Sinclair's work is adapted by Kuper, the industry's most subversive social analyst, in a kaleidoscopic art style that captures the chaos of Rudkus's world. This is American tragedy on a mythological scale, often difficult to read (on an emotional level), but as powerful and rewarding (and informative) as it was more than a hundred years ago.

*Spiegelman, Art. *The Complete Maus: A Survivor's Tale.* Pantheon, 1996.

Genre: biography, war and consequences
Discussion Topics: family issues, politics, prejudice, racial/ethnic identity, war, world history

A young man comes to terms with his father and his family history, even as his father's story of internment in the Nazi concentration camp, Auschwitz, unfolds. Underscoring the themes of racial predators and prey, Spiegelman depicts Jews as mice and Nazis as cats. This book collects *Volume 1: My Father Bleeds History* and *Volume 2: And Here My Troubles Began.*

This is the GN that got the form recognized by the world at large as a medium that could educate, enlighten, and have at its heart the deepest literary and human concerns. Its 1992 Pulitzer (upon the second volume's publication) didn't hurt at all. There is little to say about this book that hasn't already been expounded upon, and it is still the only GN that you regularly see in school curricula. It's worth noting, though, that in addition to being a powerful examination of both the dynamic between specific humans and the dynamic between humanity itself, with its use of "animal" characters, this is also a powerful comment on the very form itself.

Urasawa, Naoki. Pluto: Urasawa x Tezuka series. VIZ Media, 2009–2010.

Genre: science fiction
Discussion Topics: family issues, prejudice, war

Someone is murdering the greatest robots on Earth. A detective, who may be one of those robots himself, is charged with investigating the case, which goes far deeper down the rabbit hole than anyone suspected.

Among the great manga of all time, one of the form's current guiding lights (Urasawa) adapts and expands a tale told by one of its progenitors (Tezuka, creator of Astro Boy). Both a complicated mystery and a mind-bending sci-fi adventure, it turns out to be an intense character study as well. The detective's investigation of the other robotic life forms and his examination of his own life shed light on that perennial trope of science fiction literature: "what it is to be human."

Vaughan, Brian K. *Pride of Baghdad.* Vertigo, 2008.

Genre: war and consequences
Discussion Topics: family issues, war, world history

Vaughan's story is inspired by a true event—the bombing of Baghdad in 2003, when a zoo's worth of animals escaped their cages and roamed the city. A pride of lions wanders the ruined city, trying to survive the consequences of man's destruction.

Vaughan uses the talking animal device to its greatest effect, turning the animals' journey into a heartbreaking metaphor for life in a war zone.

*Vaughan, Brian K. Runaways series. Marvel Comics, 2003–.

Genre: superhero
Discussion Topics: coming-of-age, dating and relationships, family issues, gender roles, life skills, racial/ethnic identity, sexual orientation

A group of children get together every year when their parents have their annual meeting at an isolated estate. This year, though, the kids are old enough to get curious and uncover a life-changing secret: their parents are actually supervillains, bent on world domination. As the kids go on the run, their own burgeoning superpowers begin to develop and their journey becomes one of learning who they are as well as escaping the clutches of their past.

Vaughan has created the ultimate in coming-of-age superhero reads for teens, using the ingenious concept of the parents as supervillains to bring forward the teen experience of separating from family and facing the world on one's own. As the series progresses over multiple volumes, the journey becomes increasingly complex both in events and in moral implications. Shocking betrayals and deaths keep interest high. If you're going for only one volume, start at the beginning with the first hardcover collection, *Runaways, Volume 1.*

*Yang, Gene Luen. *American Born Chinese*. First Second, 2007.

Genre: fantasy, humor
Discussion Topics: dating and relationships, life skills, prejudice, racial/ethnic identity

Three stories unfold, intercut with one another. In the first, Jin, a Chinese student dealing with the casual prejudice of his classmates and a crush on a popular Caucasian girl, ends up betraying the trust of his one true friend. In the second, popular student Danny, who is as white-bread as they come and appears to live in a TV sitcom, must deal with the visit of a Chinese cousin, Chin-Kee, a composite of every vile and offensive Chinese stereotype imaginable. The third narrative follows the Monkey King of Chinese folklore, who has attained great power but believes that the gods are still holding him back because of what they perceive as his lowly status. Disconnected and disparate though they appear, the stories turn out to share a most unexpected and enlightening connection.

Yang's subtle, deceptive masterpiece was the first graphic novel to ever be nominated for the National Book Award, and it's not hard to see why. Using classic comic book conventions both in story construction and layout, and going for a deep irony by presenting the dark and troubling themes with the liveliest palate of colors in the most energetic style, Yang confronts some of the humanity's darker traits head on. More remarkable still is that he sheds a light of uncommon wisdom and insight on them by using the form's most overtly "childish" rudiments, showing the lie in both racial stereotyping and criticism of the sequential art form in one fell swoop. Seldom have the mechanics of the form been put to such wily use to effect such a powerful message.

GRADES 11-12

B., David. *Epileptic*. Pantheon, 2005.

Genre: biography
Discussion Topics: arts, family issues, illness, sexuality

A boy's relationship with his older brother changes when the older boy is diagnosed with epilepsy. As the disease takes a toll on the entire family, the younger brother uses art to stabilize himself.

This autobiography, imported from France, has much in common with *Maus* in its stark black-and-white art and its journey through the family's history. The role of art and dreams in the author's life lends power to a surreal sensibility, which conveys visually the author's sense of uncertainty. The jarring contrast between the brother as a boy and as a man is quite affecting.

Baker, Kyle. *King David*. Vertigo, 2002.

Genre: biography
Discussion Topics: family issues, politics, religion, sexuality, war, world history

The legendary battle with Goliath is only the beginning, as we follow King David through war, marriage, and fatherhood.

Besides depicting what is perhaps the most famous battle in human consciousness, Baker explores the burdens of leadership, the way they can corrupt a man and his commitment to his god, his family, and his people. Exaggerated colors, stylized figures, and a brand of wild humor imbue a solemn historical epic with a pulsing, chaotic life. Although this is out of print, it is still available from various online sources.

Baker, Kyle. *Nat Turner*. Abrams, 2008.

Genre: biography
Discussion Topics: prejudice, racial/ethnic identity, U.S. history

A recounting of the slave uprising of 1831, led by the young Turner, which resulted in the murder of more than fifty slave owners and their families.

Baker, one of sequential art's great historians and satirists, makes spare use of words but employs headlines and historical texts to evoke the time in question. Turner as a man and catalyst of history is examined in a balanced light, as are the hideous practices of slavery and the brutal murders of those who were on the receiving end of the slaves' wrath. An accurate and important handling of the material but absolutely not for readers who want a veil between themselves and some of history's real horrors.

Bechdel, Alison. *Fun Home: A Family Tragicomic*. Mariner Books, 2007.

Genre: biography
Discussion Topics: careers, family issues, life skills, sexual orientation, sexuality

Growing up with a father who was a closeted gay man who worked as both an English teacher and local mortician, Bechdel feels her own burgeoning lesbianism and the exploration of her teen years overshadowed. As her father and the eventual consequences of his actions slowly smother the family, Bechdel analyzes the undercurrents in hindsight.

The author-illustrator of the *Dykes to Watch Out For* strip, Bechdel has a natural voice (and a powerful memory, apparently) and well-considered thoughts on a sensitive subject. Her own story of a dysfunctional family and a torturous coming into her own as a lesbian offers a great deal of wisdom on those subjects and many others.

Book of Genesis. **Adapted by Robert Crumb. W. W. Norton, 2009.**

Genre: literary adaptation
Discussion Topics: family issues, religion, world history

The entire first book of the Bible, from the creation of the universe to the death of Joseph, with Cain and Abel, Noah and the flood, and about eight million "begats" along the way.

Underground icon Crumb, famed for his disdain for authority and often misogynist depictions of sexuality, may seem an odd artist to have taken on this project, but his handling is effective and, at times, potent. His rough-hewn cartoon faces and bodies give the stories a very human grounding, and the sexuality and violence are presented frankly but tastefully. He also has a remarkable talent for creating distinctive faces, which comes in handy when you have to go through a page full of head shots for the numerous lineages that appear. The Bible, of course, is rife with drama, pathos, and wonder, and Crumb, a master of the form whatever else you may want to say about him, knows how to use sequential art's strengths to take full advantage.

Busiek, Kurt. *Marvels.* Marvel Comics, 1995.

Genre: superhero
Discussion Topics: prejudice, U.S. history, war

Phil Sheldon is a photographer for the *Daily Bugle,* who documents the actions (and consequences of those actions) of superheroes and supervillains. From World War II through the antimutant hysteria and alien invasions of later days, the story traces Marvel superhero history (and actual world history) from the viewpoint of the common man.

An excellent companion piece to *Kingdom Come* (included in this list), also featuring Ross's dynamic but deeply humanized and realistic art, *Marvels* also tackles the question of what effects the powerful have on the vulnerable. Busiek creates a compelling sweep of history. By adopting a normal person's point of view and witnessing epic, city-crushing, hero-villain clashes as well as inspiring deeds of selfless sacrifice, the story highlights the extraordinary actions even the most ordinary among us are capable of.

Carey, Mike. The Unwritten series. Vertigo, 2010–.

Genre: adventure, fantasy
Discussion Topics: art history (literature), dating and relationships, family issues, life skills, popular culture, world history

Tommy Taylor's father wrote a runaway best-selling series of fantasy novels about a young wizard and his friends fighting terrible evil and based the main character on Tommy himself. Now that his father has disappeared and is presumed dead, Tommy ekes out a rather pathetic living with convention tours and bookstore appearances. When someone tries to reveal him as a fake, he finds himself not only caught up in an ancient conspiracy, but also on the trail of a secret so powerful it will change Tommy's understanding of his own nature forever.

Uncommonly smart and highly literate, this is a heady mix of historical literary allusions, pop culture commentary, and complex thriller. Tommy's history alternates with details of the conspiracy as they manipulate some of the greatest imaginations in history, including Rudyard Kipling and Mark Twain.

Chadwick, Paul. Concrete series. Dark Horse, 1987–.

Genre: realistic fiction, science fiction
Discussion Topics: dating and relationships, life skills, sexuality

Ronald Lithgow's mind has been placed into the superpowerful body of a massive, mobile, stonelike monolith. But rather than fighting crime, he takes road trips and writes about his experiences, to help him deal with what he has lost and explore what still remains.

One of independent comics' earliest gems, *Concrete* takes elements, rules, and tropes of superhero comics and ignores them completely. Lithgow may have been imbued with extraordinary powers by an alien race, but his adventures are almost exclusively of the mind and the heart, dealing with friendship and love from an unwilling outsider's point of view. Chadwick uses his fanciful premise to explore human nature in intelligent, perceptive, melancholy, and joyful ways. Absolutely start at the beginning of the series with *Concrete, Volume 1: Depths*.

Clowes, Daniel. *Ghost World*. Fantagraphics Books, 2001.

Genre: realistic fiction
Discussion Topics: coming-of-age, dating and relationships, gender roles, life skills, sexual orientation, sexuality

Enid and Rebecca are longtime friends who have just graduated from high school and find their paths diverging. Enid plans to leave the working-class neighborhood she grew up in and go to college, and she is spending time with an older man whom she herself describes as a creep and a pervert. Meanwhile, Rebecca has taken up with quiet Josh, once the target of the girls' hectoring, and seems headed for a "normal" life in their nowhere, nothing little town.

This book in many ways defined the indie comics scene when it was first published (collected, actually, having first appeared serially in Clowes's *Eightball*) in the early 1990s. It is rife with cynicism, dirty language, and a painfully realistic take on life after high school.

Eisner, Will. *A Contract with God and Other Tenement Stories.* Baronet Books, 1978.

Genre: realistic fiction
Discussion Topics: coming-of-age, dating and relationships, family issues, religion, racial/ethnic identity, sexuality, socioeconomic class, U.S. history

Four short stories expound on life in a Bronx tenement in the 1930s. They include a boy (and later adult) who makes a deal with God, an out-of-work bookkeeper who becomes a street singer but through the apparent good graces of a stranger spirals ever downward, a cautionary tale about an authoritarian German superintendent who gives in to the wrong kind of temptation, and a trip to a Jewish resort community in the Adirondacks that focuses on the need to get ahead and how to do it (or how not to).

This is not technically the first GN, but it is the first work to employ that term and the first to tell a nongenre story that focused on the ordeals that human nature can produce for itself, specifically encompassed by the social class and culture of the author's childhood. Eisner is the quintessential master (he even invented the term *sequential art*). His images are filled with character and pathos, his composition is inventive and flows beautifully, and his stories possess an undeniable and compelling insight.

Forman, Ari. *Waltz with Bashir: A Lebanon War Story*. Metropolitan Books, 2009.

Genre: war and consequences
Discussion Topics: politics, war, world history

Years after he fought in Lebanon, a former soldier begins to experience horrific dreams that suggest buried memories of his time at war. He begins visiting other members of his unit to uncover the mystery, though the truth may be more than he can handle.

Wrapped in a mystery that draws readers in, and illustrated in a unique animated form (the style of the animated movie upon which it's based), *Waltz with Bashir* sheds light on the atrocities that war pushes men into and what the men sometimes do to deal with it.

Gaiman, Neil. Sandman series. Vertigo, 1993–.

Genre: fantasy
Discussion Topics: family issues, sexuality, world history

In ten volumes (if you choose the trade collections), we follow Morpheus, the Lord of Dreams and one of the seven Endless, a family of godlike beings who personify various abstract concepts (such as Destiny, Death, and Desire—yes, all their names begin with *D*). Morpheus weaves his way through the imaginings of mortals and touches them in ways ranging from the sublime to the terrifying. The stories feature a wide array of characters, including some obscure DC Comics staples and even William Shakespeare.

This series launched Gaiman's stratospheric career, mixing fantasy and horror in an epic series that often feels positively literary and that pushed the frontiers of what comics were allowed to be.

Gaiman, Neil. *Sandman: The Dream Hunters*. Adapted by P. Craig Russel. Vertigo, 2009.

Genre: fantasy
Discussion Topics: dating and relationships, gender roles, sexuality

In old Japan, a wily fox makes a wager with a young monk but finds herself bound to him in ways she never imagined. Their bond provokes the interest of a demon lord and, ultimately, the intervention of Morpheus, the Lord of Dreams.

Of all the various offshoots the series produced, this is the most lyrical and lovely. Although the tale springs completely from the author's mind, it is told so convincingly in the style of a Japanese folktale and illustrated with such care and stylistic respect that you will swear you're reading an ancient manuscript. The Morpheus character is woven fluidly into a tale of deep love and commitment.

Gipi. *Garage Band*. First Second, 2007.

Genre: realistic fiction
Discussion Topics: arts (music), coming-of-age, life skills

Four directionless boys come together to make music, but when a real opportunity arises, they clash and a dreadful mistake dooms their effort. In the end, however, some are still left with a touch of hope.

Italian writer-artist Gipi tells a complex story of friendship and choices with simple sweeps of plot and dialogue, and jittery, indie-inspired art that captures a sense of tension and uncertainty. He also portrays, with ringing success, the potent joy of music in a non-audio medium.

Homer. *The Odyssey*. Adapted by Gareth Hinds. Candlewick, 2010.

Genre: literary adaptation, mythology
Discussion Topics: art history (literature), family issues, politics, war, world history

More complete and realistic than the All-Action Classic version (listed in the previous chapter), this lavish retelling of Odysseus's journey home isn't afraid to take its time in building characters and political tension between the gods before blasting into its epic action. The hero's intelligence and guile are honored over his physical strength, and the trials have never seemed more punishing or genuine.

The stunningly rendered art—evoking every texture and color of the era—lends an unusual level of realism that strengthens the exploration of a war veteran's inner world and the ties he has to his family.

Jacobson, Sid. *The 9/11 Report: A Graphic Adaptation*. Hill and Wang, 2006.

Genre: nonfiction
Discussion Topics: politics, terrorism, U.S. history

Jacobson translates the actual commission findings into sequential narrative, reporting on causes, the event itself, and its ramifications.

This sober, factual, unsensational adaptation opens the report up to a wide array of readers it would never have reached otherwise. A unique experiment capitalizing on the form's great strength of accessibility.

*Kelly, Joe. *I Kill Giants*. Image Comics, 2009.

Genre: fantasy, realistic fiction
Discussion Topics: illness, life skills, mental health

Barbara Thorson is a little girl with a big hammer who claims that she is preparing for battle with a terrifying giant. Or is this all a matter of an emotional imbalance brought on by family issues?

As it turns out, Barbara has both emotional problems and a terrifying giant to battle. This could easily have been a rather tasteless look at mental difficulties, but it instead combines an engaging mythological adventure with a sympathetic look at childhood and its tragedies.

Kirkman, Robert. Walking Dead series. Image Comics, 2004–.

Genre: horror, realistic fiction
Discussion Topics: dating and relationships, family issues, gender roles, illness, life skills, mental health, racial/ethnic identity, religion

When the world is overrun by zombies, a policeman takes his wife and son on a journey across country to find some kind of a future. Their journey takes them through many twists and turns, and the story acquires a cast of characters whose realism and depth have seldom been rivaled in comics.

Kirkman's far-reaching and intensely layered story and characterizations make for addictive reading, and his surprises are so gut-wrenching you quickly learn that nothing (and no character) is sacred. As with the best zombie horror, the walking dead are used as an opportunity to examine society and what holds it together. Kirkman goes further still by making his characters so recognizable and distinctive; at the same time, he has created horror on a grand scale that offers far more than a simple thrill ride. Caution: the series has produced eleven volumes as of this writing with no ending in sight. You can safely buy the first three volumes and, while it's clear the story has plenty left to go, your readers won't feel cheated.

Lethem, Jonathan. *Omega the Unknown*. Marvel Comics, 2009.

Genre: realistic fiction, superhero
Discussion Topics: life skills, racial/ethnic identity

After a terrible accident, a boy learns that his recently deceased parents were actually robots and that something very strange seems to be hunting him. Protected by a mysterious, silent guardian, the boy and his friends seek the truth of his history, working against—among other assorted and deeply weird menaces—a snide celebrity superhero for hire.

Novelist Lethem layers his story with questions of identity and creates believable and compelling teen characters struggling with realistic issues in the midst of all the postmodern strangeness. It is the most honest depiction of inner-city schools and teen life found in a superhero comic. Do not confuse this with the collection on which it was based, an obscure title from the 1970s called *Omega the Unknown Classic,* by Steve Gerber and Jim Mooney.

Millar, Mark. *Superman: Red Son*. DC Comics, 2004.

Genre: superhero
Discussion Topics: politics, world history

Rocketed from the planet Krypton before it was destroyed, the baby who would become Superman crash-landed in a small midwestern town and was adopted by a humble farm family who taught him the American values of responsibility and community service. But what if, instead of Smallville, Kansas, the rocket had crash-landed in Soviet Russia? What if the boy was inculcated into Stalinist Communism? What impact would that have on world politics and the future of the planet?

The alternate version of the familiar hero (as well as several others, including Batman and Green Lantern) and his impact on the course of human events offers insight not only into the politics of another culture, but also into many of the things about our own culture that we take for granted.

Miller, Frank. *Dark Knight Returns*. DC Comics, 1986.

Genre: superhero
Discussion Topics: politics

An aging Bruce Wayne sees Gotham City falling apart around him, the prey of ultraviolent gangs and political indifference. Donning the Batman costume once again, he finds a new Robin and faces down his enemies and the United States government itself.

Along with *Watchmen* and *Maus,* this book was single-handedly (or triple-handedly, really) responsible for the maturation and mainstreaming of sequential art and GNs. Mainly a political satire of Reagan-era America and consumer culture in general, the book makes its point in large strokes, ultimately pitting the dark but humanist Batman against a gleaming, invincible Superman, recast as the symbol of America's smiling, empty-headed complacency. Very violent but with a hard-core political agenda seldom found in mainstream comics.

Miller, Frank. *300.* Dark Horse, 1999.

Genre: war and consequences
Discussion Topics: politics, war, world history

The battle of Thermopylae pitted 300 Spartans against a hundreds-of-thousands-strong Persian army in a battle that the rest of Greece didn't dare fight. The indomitable character of the people in history's quintessential soldier-tribe is given human qualities in the form of their leader, King Leonidas, staunch and courageous and as humane as they came back in Sparta, and also in the pain of the eager but misshapen Ephialtes, who must weather ridicule and disrespect and is ultimately driven to take unfortunate steps.

Miller researched his history well. Although some of the cultural references seem anachronistic, the logistics of the politics and the battle are dead center. As a veteran of many of comicdom's most crushingly violent and socially aware comics (most notably the seminal *Dark Knight Returns,* included in this list), Miller handles both the action and the character interactions exceedingly well. With his figure work reminiscent of a comic book Francis Bacon and his spare and evocative environments, his art proves a perfect match for this gritty, bone-crunching historical drama.

Milligan, Peter. *X-Force: Famous, Mutant, and Mortal.* Marvel Comics, 2003.

Genre: superhero
Discussion Topics: dating and relationships, gender roles, life skills, popular culture, racial/ethnic identity

Instead of going into hiding as the X-Men do, a group of young mutants use their powers and oddities to make themselves into huge celebrities. But even with the X-Force media machine behind them, there are deadly menaces gunning for them.

Deconstructing the superhero, Milligan uses the comic book platform to put media hypocrisy on trial by turning Marvel's hated minorities into celebrities loved and pursued by the world. The pressures of such attention and notoriety cause predictable—but nonetheless engaging and insightful—dissension within their ranks.

*Moore, Alan. *Watchmen.* DC Comics, 1986.

Genre: realistic fiction, superhero
Discussion Topics: gender roles, family issues, life skills, mental health, politics, sexuality, war, U.S. history

In an alternate 1985 America where Nixon is still president and tension with the Soviets has reached disastrous levels, a group of outlaw superheroes come out of retirement to find the murderer who's hunting them, but they also uncover a plot of global proportions.

Moore's literary portrayal of realistically troubled (and troubling) characters and world politics at the brink, along with Gibbons's mastery and subtle reinventions of the art form, have earned this book a reputation as the greatest GN ever created (just consult *Time*'s All-Time 100 Novels list). At any rate, it was a watershed moment in the evolution of the industry, codifying all the themes and techniques that had been laid out chaotically before and paving a road that every comic book afterward would tread.

*Morrell, David. *Captain America: The Chosen*. Marvel Comics, 2008.

Genre: war and consequences
Discussion Topics: life skills, war

A dying Captain America tries to bequeath a final legacy to a young solider fighting in Iraq who is plagued by self-doubt and trapped in a deadly situation.

Along with *Civil War* (cited earlier), this is a grand example of the expansive possibilities of the superhero genre and its ability to address modern social issues. You might expect a less-thoughtful consideration of the problems of war and conflict from novelist Morrell, who created the character of Rambo, but this is anything but a glorification, focusing instead on the significance of role models and the potential of every person to be a hero.

*Neufeld, Josh. *A.D.: New Orleans after the Deluge*. Pantheon, 2009.

Genre: nonfiction
Discussion Topics: family issues, politics, prejudice, U.S. history

Six stories, based on interviews with survivors of Hurricane Katrina, detail the lives of people from the hours before the storm hit New Orleans to the days following. From the wait atop a submerged house for a rescue that may never come, to the realization that a lifetime's worth of treasured possessions has been lost forever, to the nightmare of the superdome, the dilemmas, choices, and lack of choices these people are confronted with often hit as hard as the hurricane itself.

The GN form exhibits its potential for timeliness by being among the first formats to so trenchantly examine such a tragic piece of recent history. No melodrama or exaggerated circumstances here—just true, painful, and unforgettable demonstrations of the courage with which many faced the ruins of their lives, and the government's astonishing and appalling failure to help them.

Pak, Greg. *X-Men: Magneto Testament*. Marvel Comics, 2009.

Genre: war and consequences
Discussion Topics: coming-of-age, dating and relationships, politics, prejudice, racial/ ethnic identity, war, world history

Max Eisenhardt lives a life of tragedy and struggle as he sees his parents gunned down by German soldiers as they flee the invasion of Poland in 1935. Max works to escape the concentration camp he is taken prisoner in, along with the Gypsy girl whom, in a simpler time, he would be able to love.

The corporate agenda behind attaching the X-Men brand to an intelligently and unsparingly told story about the Holocaust smacks of the worst sort of commercialism. It's not that superheroes can't be used to tell important, serious stories, but that here the X-Men name is stamped onto a story that has nothing to do with and *needs* nothing to do with the characters. Even the character of Max, the future Magneto himself, is essentially just a normal (if courageous and dogged) young man. One should want to dismiss this book out of hand simply for Marvel's marketing cynicism. But the problem is that Pak tells an incredibly intelligent, impeccably researched story that is loaded with emotion due to its setting, and he treats the events with the utmost gravity and respect. This book is, in many ways, an ideal teaching tool for this period of history and in fact includes an extensive teacher's guide for just such a purpose. Although it is hard to ignore the presence of the brand (or erase the knowledge of it from your students), looking past it is necessary in order to reap the considerable benefits of such a powerfully told and well-conceived tale that gives its subject its due.

Powell, Nate. *Swallow Me Whole*. Top Shelf Productions, 2008.

Genre: realistic fiction
Discussion Topics: family issues, mental health

Ruth and Perry are teen stepsiblings who both have mental disorders. Ruth has OCD and schizophrenia, which engenders an obsession with insects that leads to fixations and troubling dreams, and Perry cannot seem to control a fantasy figure that causes a mania for creating art.

Portrayed in the most realistic terms and featuring a family that is both loving and believable, *Swallow Me Whole* uses the troubled teens' own inner life and perspective to create a deeply affecting and sympathetic portrait.

Rucka, Greg, and J. H. Williams. *Batwoman: Elegy*. DC Comics, 2010.

Genre: superhero
Discussion Topics: arts (visual), dating and relationships, family issues, gender roles, life skills, sexual orientation, sexuality

Batwoman (not to be confused with Batgirl) is Katherine Kane, ex-military, current protector of Gotham City. In the first arc of the collection, she takes on the ghoulish new High Madame of the Religion of Crime. In the second arc, we look back into Kane's origins as her strength and commitment are formed by a childhood trauma that occurred while she was moving around the world as an Army brat. Having enlisted in the military herself, she leaves it behind when she is told she must deny allegations that she is a lesbian.

A valuable and powerful read not only for the second arc's social relevance and Batwoman's prominence as a homosexual superhero, but also because the sharp writing is matched with art so jaw-dropping in its design and figural craft as to be unique within the history of mainstream comics. Combat depicted within lightning bolts that flash across the pages, word balloons that visually match the character speaking, and an homage to a seminal Batman story of the past (*Batman: Year One*, a retelling of the hero's origin by Frank Miller and David Mazzucchelli) just scratch the surface of this breathtaking artistic achievement.

*Satrapi, Marjane. *The Complete Persepolis*. Pantheon, 2007.

Genre: biography
Discussion Topics: coming-of-age, family issues, gender roles, life skills, politics, prejudice, racial/ethnic identity, religion, world history

Satrapi tells her story of growing up in Iran as the daughter of intellectual dissidents during the Islamic Revolution and the consequent reinstatement of a religious government. As she grows up, she travels through Europe, pushing the boundaries set for her by the expectations of herself and others, and she reconciles her past and her future. This volume compiles *Persepolis: The Story of a Childhood* and *Persepolis 2: The Story of a Return*.

Satrapi's memoir is a well-deserved classic, a pioneer of the sequential art style that couples deceptively simple, childlike drawings with a story that explores intense and controversial themes. While the ruminations on religious repression and war make specific and larger points about the world, Satrapi's life as a young woman fascinated by the West and struggling against the limits of her culture and upbringing will be immediately accessible to teen readers.

Shakespeare, William. *Merchant of Venice.* Adapted by Gareth Hinds. Candlewick, 2008.

Genre: literary adaptation
Discussion Topics: art history (literature), dating and relationships, prejudice, socioeconomic class, world history

Hinds's *King Lear* is extremely accomplished, but his *Merchant of Venice* is a more frankly fascinating take on Shakespeare, as Hinds tends to eschew the ostensible comedy and invites readers to wrestle with the play's more contemporarily controversial aspects, also reflected with thick lines, gray tones, and snatches of contemporary English. A powerful, if not definitive, adaptation.

Of all the GN Shakespeare adaptations, Hinds's characters are the most well defined and expressive and his art the most subtle and beautiful to look at. His work is highly recommended for those reading for pleasure or for a sense of the more conceptual aspects of Shakespeare's work (its spirit, if you will).

Shanower, Eric. Age of Bronze series. Image Comics, 2001–.

Genre: war and consequences
Discussion Topics: family issues, politics, sexuality, war, world history

Projected to be seven volumes when complete (and currently at three), Shanower's work tells a vast tale of intertwining dramas ranging from the highest levels of royalty to the lowest soldiers, recounting the Trojan War with heavily researched, accurate detail and stuffed to the gills with intrigue, betrayal, battle, love, and death.

Age of Bronze is the standard by which all historical GNs (and for that matter novels) about the time period should be measured. Shanower's research is worthy of a scholarly treatise; his grasp of the political and human forces of the time is insightful, and the information woven seamlessly into his riveting story equals that of most textbooks on the subject.

Sikoryak, R. *Masterpiece Comics.* Drawn and Quarterly, 2009.

Genre: literary adaptation
Discussion Topics: art history (literature), religion, sexuality, world history

Blondie and Dagwood are in Genesis, Garfield is seen through the eyes of Dante, Little Lulu wears the shame of the scarlet letter, Batman faces crime and punishment, and Superman lives the existentially meaningless life envisioned by Albert Camus. These are but a few of the adaptations of classic literature told with the characters from, and in the style of, classic comic books.

Sikoryak's understanding of literature's deeper themes mixes with his uncanny ability to mimic the styles of many of comic history's greatest artists and produces far more than a hilarious satire. By honoring the past of both, he brings to the surface the themes that have resonated throughout history in all forms of expression and offers a fascinating look at how humans convey stories.

Silady, Matt. *The Homeless Channel.* AiT/Planet Lar, 2007.

Genre: realistic fiction

Discussion Topics: careers, dating and relationships, family issues, gender roles, popular culture, sexuality, socioeconomic class

Darcy Shaw has come up with the newest, hottest idea for a reality TV show: 24-hour coverage of homeless people; interviews, trailing them around, full coverage of their lives. Things begin to fall apart, however, when the homeless situation hits close to home, as Darcy's sister finds herself out on the streets.

Silady asks some interesting questions about both the power of media and the nation's socioeconomic problems and couches the controversy in a setting teens will be intimately familiar with: the reality TV show.

Simmons, Josh. *House.* Fantagraphics, 2007.

Genre: horror

Discussion Topics: language arts

In this wordless tale, three teens meet in the woods and go exploring, until they find an abandoned, partially submerged house that delivers them to their slow, agonizing fate.

The story of an evil place couldn't be simpler or more classic, but Simmons's art makes the piece simply astonishing. The intricate black-and-white illustration reveals rising jealousy between the teens and their mounting terror as the house becomes a trap. The transition from light to shadow spells the imminent and unavoidable doom that is the hallmark of the most effective horror. Most of all, the page composition and panel size create both a sense of vast possibility and mystery in full double-page spreads, and claustrophobic, inescapable fear as the panels become smaller and smaller, closing in on the doomed teens. Not just excellent horror, but a visual tour de force that uses the tools of sequential art to inspired effect.

Small, David. *Stitches: A Memoir.* W. W. Norton, 2009.

Genre: biography

Discussion Topics: family issues, illness, mental health, sexual orientation

Small grows up in a house dominated by parental cruelty. The father, a radiologist whose carelessness may have caused his son's cancer, and the mother, filled with harsh resentment of her son and her place in life, are the two monsters that the author spends his entire life running from, at least up to its hopeful ending.

Small captures the child's-eye view to great effect, showing us the faith he put in his parents at the same time that we see how their gross and bitter negligence could easily have destroyed him. A picture book illustrator, Small's imagery captures a jittery world where darkness always seems to be closing in and every face seems to stare down with anger. A harrowing and painful tale, winner of multiple awards, it does not leave the reader without hope, but it does not undercut its own darkness either.

Sturm, James. *James Sturm's America: God, Gold, and Golems.* **Drawn and Quarterly, 2007.**

Genre: realistic fiction
Discussion Topics: family issues, racial/ethnic identity, socioeconomic class, U.S. history

The opportunity for a new life is offered to frontier settlers by a religious revival, and the lure of gold gives high but false hopes. This pair of vignettes serves as an appetizer to *The Golem's Mighty Swing,* a full-length story that details the journey of a Jewish baseball team and the captain who struggles to keep them together with a plan to attract audiences via the promise of a golem (an ancient creature of clay spoken of in Jewish folklore) taking the field.

Sturm is a historian, baseball lover (his *Satchel Paige: Striking Out Jim Crow* is on the younger reader's list), and the GN world's premiere humanist observer of historical currents. His keen sense of time and place and his insight into the hopes that drive human beings raise his stories of the role of hucksterism in the formation of American culture to a literary level.

Tamaki, Mariko. *Skim.* **Groundwood Books, 2008.**

Genre: realistic fiction
Discussion Topics: coming-of-age, life skills, racial/ethnic identity, sexual orientation, sexuality

Pudgy Asian American student Skim is poorly treated by fellow students in her all-girl school. Her anguish is exacerbated by her briefly requited love for a female drama teacher.

The writing and art are drenched in a very realistic sense of pain and teen nihilism and, though it courts several controversial issues (including a relationship between a teacher and student), it is one of the few works in the genre that confronts the question of sexual orientation so skillfully.

Thompson, Craig. *Blankets.* **Top Shelf Productions, 2003.**

Genre: realistic fiction
Discussion Topics: coming-of-age, dating and relationships, family issues, life skills, religion, sexuality

Thompson's epic (592 pages) recounting of growing up in a fundamentalist Christian household, from his parents' painfully restrictive philosophy to the desperate bond between himself and his younger brother to the wonder and longing of discovering first love.

Blankets made Thompson something of an indie god, and deservedly so. Seldom have art and words meshed so well, their unity building a story filled with the melancholy of growing up.

Van Lente, Fred. *Action Philosophers! The More than Complete Edition.* **Evil Twin Comics, 2009.**

Genre: biography
Discussion Topics: religion, world history

In this surprisingly complete survey of philosophers throughout the ages, each issue (or chapter in this collected form) is devoted to a general theme, such as fathers of philosophy

(Plato, Bodhidharma, and Nietzsche), psychologist philosophers (Freud, Jung, and Campbell), political philosophers (Machiavelli, Marx, and the Kabbalah), and French philosophers (Descartes, Sartre, and Derrida).

Rather dense text and dialogue give a detailed account of the particular philosopher's life, or her philosophy, and the attitudes and the environment that shaped him or her (Ayn Rand is one of the few females included). This exhaustively researched information is coupled with often hilarious imagery that illustrates some surprising information about many of these hallowed thinkers (Plato's career as a wrestler, Joseph Campbell's philosophy of the heroic journey being co-opted by comic book fans) or satirizes their philosophy in the form's unique idiom (Husserl takes up extreme skateboarding; "Wicked awesome, dude!" cries Descartes). This is a classic example of sneaking education in on a platform of great hilarity and fun.

Vaughan, Brian K. Y: The Last Man series. Vertigo, 2003–2008.

Genre: science fiction
Discussion Topics: coming-of-age, dating and relationships, gender roles, family issues, politics, racial/ethnic identity, religion, sexuality

Yorick Brown, escape artist in training and good-natured all-around slacker, walks out of his apartment one day to find that a mysterious virus has killed every human being on the planet with a Y chromosome—except him. What follows is the greatest epic journey in modern comics, as Yorick traverses an Earth slowly rebuilding itself, with a secret agent, a scientist, and his pet monkey, searching for the cause of this collapse and for Yorick's lost love.

For believable, sympathetic characters, riveting situations, and grand, highly intelligent speculation in the best science fiction tradition, this may be the best comic series ever produced. The relationship between Yorick and his erstwhile companions and his ponderings over being the last man alive are balanced with supposition of what a world without men would be like. That question serves to illuminate exactly how our world works now, with all its advantages and shortcomings.

*Waid, Mark. *Kingdom Come*. DC Comics, 1997.

Genre: superhero, war and consequences
Discussion Topics: gender roles, life skills, politics, religion, war

In the future, after all the familiar DC superheroes have retired, a new breed of ultraviolent heroes accidentally causes a devastating nuclear explosion within the United States. Superman attempts to rally the older heroes to confront these unrepentant new guardians. But is the world ready to accept Superman's antiquated morality?

This gigantic, ambitious, epic superhero drama asks penetrating questions about inspiration, role models, religion, trust, and when, if ever, is the right time to engage in war. Waid weaves powerful themes into an exciting tale of intrigue and conflicting moral outlooks, and Ross's gorgeous, painted, hyperrealistic art lends the book a superior sense of reality and makes this story an archetypal superhero tale for the ages.

Waid, Mark. *Superman: Birthright*. DC Comics, 2005.

Genre: superhero
Discussion Topics: coming-of-age, gender roles, life skills, politics, racial/ethnic identity, war

Clark Kent departs Smallville to experience the world, but the soon-to-be Superman gets embroiled in politics and war in Africa. He carries hard-learned lessons with him to Metropolis, where he confronts Lex Luthor, who has gained control of Superman's legacy, which he uses to attack not only the hero, but also his burgeoning reputation.

A slightly harder-edged look at the Superman mythology, concentrating on years of the character's life that are seldom touched on. Waid does an excellent job of portraying an innocent farm boy's difficult acquisition of uncomfortable wisdom and then pits him against a singularly insidious Lex Luthor. Using Superman's own heritage against him proves a potent metaphor for facing and overcoming one's own past.

Ware, Chris. *Jimmy Corrigan, the Smartest Kid on Earth.* Pantheon, 2003.

Genre: realistic fiction
Discussion Topics: arts (visual), family issues, life skills, mental health, sexuality

In daily life and flashback, we are acquainted with Jimmy Corrigan, a chubby, defeated, middle-aged loser, as he prepares for a reunion with the father who abandoned him in childhood. The meeting, not unexpectedly, brings a whole new level of despair.

Ware's background in graphic design results in a GN that looks like no other. The composition of the pages, panels, and visual story as a whole, combined with the exacting and highly stylized figural work, produces a unique work of art. The story itself is about regret, defeat, and desolation and is for mature teens prepared to read what very well may be (I'm not kidding here) the most depressing book ever written.

*Weing, Drew. *Set to Sea.* Fantagraphics Books, 2010.

Genre: adventure
Discussion Topics: arts, careers, coming-of-age, life skills, socioeconomic class

A big galoot who dreams of becoming a poet finds, instead, the rigors of a hard life at sea. Amidst the labor and tumult he accrues a lifetime's worth of hard-won wisdom and a touch of the poetry he once longed for.

Weing's art is deceptively cartoonish and incredibly precise, filled with creeping, cross-hatched shadows and rendered in small, single-panel pages. It is at once an homage to Segar's *Popeye* and a glorious exploration all its own. You will not find a simpler, more powerful tale of beauty and wisdom in graphic literature (you'd be hard put to find it anywhere, in fact). That such mature depths are made accessible to teens is all the more extraordinary,

Whedon, Joss. *Buffy Season Eight* series. Dark Horse, 2007–2011.

Genre: fantasy, horror
Discussion Topics: coming-of-age, life skills, sexual orientation, sexuality

Picking up directly where the TV series about the teen vampire slayer left off, Buffy and Xander now run a training camp for slayers, where they contend with the U.S. Army, Dracula, and a mysterious uber-villian, Twilight.

All the regular character are back, and Whedon and his collaborators (both writers of the original series and various comic book luminaries) preserve the fun action, complex plots, intense emotional stakes, and thoughtful handling of teen-significant issues. Of particular note in this case is Buffy's experimentation with a same-sex relationship.

Willingham, Bill. Fables series. Vertigo, 2002–.

Genre: fairy tale/folktale, fantasy
Discussion Topics: dating and relationships, politics, sexuality

The characters of fairy tales have been forced out of their homeland and now live in a colony in New York City. But when Red Rose is apparently murdered, her boyfriend Jack (of beanstalk fame) must solve the mystery under the watchful eye of Rose's sister, the bitter, divorced, and controlling Snow White. As things proceed, the dark undercurrents of fairy tale existence start boiling to the surface. And that's just the first volume!

A great premise is played for all it's worth as Willingham builds an entire culture and world for these displaced fairy tale figures, focusing on different characters at different times and using different genres within the overall fantasy for a trenchant examination of many real-world issues. As the serialized story (and spin-offs) become increasingly complex, definitely start with volume 1, titled *Legends in Exile*.

PART FOUR

Lesson Plans and Activities

CHAPTERS 8 AND 9 PRESENT LESSON PLANS THAT ARE MEANT to help incorporate GNs into school curricula of various types, but they can be applied to library programs and discussion groups as well. Chapter 8 focuses on the form of sequential art itself—the way a specific work illuminates that form and the manner in which the form conveys narrative, theme, character, and tone uniquely and powerfully. Chapter 9 concentrates on analysis of the content of individual GNs, in the same manner one might develop a lesson around a novel.

The form has great potential in practical education, and these suggested lessons are but the tip of the iceberg. Hopefully, something in the following chapters will inspire you to develop your own lessons for your school or library.

8

LEARNING ABOUT THE FORM

THE FOLLOWING LESSON PLANS EDUCATE THROUGH THE ART of the GN and the object itself—the manner in which sequential art is produced and the final aesthetic product. The lessons include ways to involve students in sequential art through creation and study. They underscore the unique way in which this particular art form imbues a narrative with life.

The lessons are arranged by grade level. The grade range for many of the plans is quite wide because the individual lessons can easily be tailored to younger or older students.

THE BASICS

Grade Level: K–2

Goal: To understand the rudiments of sequential art sequencing and story construction.

Text Used: *The Snowman* by Raymond Briggs (see chapter 6)

Lesson: Using a ready-made but wordless sequential narrative, students can build (or rebuild) a sequence themselves and add words to help clarify the order of events.

Activity 1: Photocopy the third page of *The Snowman* (starting with the boy looking up at the blank snowman and ending with the boy looking up at the completed snowman). Cut the copied pages into their individual panels. Give a complete (though cut-apart) page to each student and allow the student to build the sequence in order. You can assist students with cues (for instance, the boy needs to get the orange before he can place it on the snowman). The sequence does not need to be in the precisely correct order, but it should make narrative sense when finished. Allow the student to explain what is happening in each panel and the chronological connection from one to the next.

Activity 2: Photocopy the three pages toward the end, beginning with the boy and the snowman sitting at the table and ending with the full-page panel of the snowman and the boy taking flight. You may repeat the preceding exercise with this sequence as well, cutting the panels apart and allowing students to order them. However, with this sequence you should also ask the students to create dialogue for each panel for the boy and the snowman. Sit with the youngest students and draw word balloons and fill in words for them by dictation. For older students, instruct them to draw word balloons and write in simple dialogue. When the students are finished, ask each one to describe what is happening on his or her pages, taking cues from the dialogue: Are the boy and the snowman excited? Are they sad? Are they friends? Where do they want to go?

IMAGES IN THE REAL WORLD

Grade Level: 1–3

Goal: To understand that imagery is part of how we understand things in real life as well as on a comic page.

Lesson: Discuss with students how images are often used to give us messages in the real world.

Activity 1: Instruct students to find an example of this over the course of a few days as homework. The images do not necessarily need to be in sequence, but they should convey a complete message. They may contain words but should not rely on them to transmit the meaning. Signage is an excellent example of this, as are instruction manuals and advertisements. Students should get a picture of the examples they find.

Students should share the images they found. Alternatively, the teacher can provide an array of examples and display them for the class. Discuss with students how each image tells us what it wants us to know. Note how many signs use codes (like the crossed circle in No Smoking signs) much as comics do.

Activity 2: Have students create a sign that conveys a message about school or classroom rules that could be posted somewhere in the classroom. The image should use no words but could use codes and may be in a sequence of up to two "panels" long.

Let students show their work and explain how they created their messages.

IMAGINATION AND STYLE

Grade Level: 1–3

Goal: To understand that there are many different ways to depict both actions and emotions in sequential art.

Lesson: Because each person's imagination and drawing style are different, no two people will conceive of and depict the same thing in the same way. Indeed, this is the very nature of creation and expression.

Activity 1: Have each student represent a figure jumping in three different ways. Students may do it in a single panel using speed lines, in two panels allowing the gutter to "hold the jump," or in any other way their imaginations conceive of;" angle, body language, and sense of motion all come into play. When they are finished, allow students to compare their images. Many will repeat, but display for the class unusual or inventive ways of putting across the idea.

Activity 2: Have each student represent the concept of sadness in three different ways. Facial expression, tears, body language (hunching), or even a word balloon with the words *I'm sad* are all possibilities. As with activity 1, allow students to compare their work and then display the most unusual depictions.

CREATING COMICS

Grade Level: 1–4

Goal: To understand the rudiments of sequential art language, codes, and symbols through creation of a comic.

Lesson: Students should be acquainted with the following rudiments of sequential art:

Panel—the box in which all action takes place.

Speech balloon—for everything spoken by a character. You can also present the thought balloon.

Symbols—speed lines, unconscious or dead eyes (*x*'s instead of dots), smell lines, impact stars. Present a small selection to choose from.

Facial expressions—extreme versions are used to convey emotions such as happiness, anger, sadness, or surprise.

Alternatively, assign or read in class *Adventures in Cartooning* (see chapter 6) for an excellent primer on the same elements.

Activity 1: Have students individually create a comic book that comprises six panels on one horizontal sheet of paper and uses the elements of sequential art listed above. The story should read as follows:

Panel 1: A person gets a letter and is very surprised. He or she can say or think something here.

Panel 2: The person runs from his or her house, prepared for a journey.

Panel 3: The person is traveling but encounters an obstacle that he or she must pass. It could be a hole, a guard, or a river—anything that requires action to navigate. The person is mad or sad to see this. He or she can say or think something here.

Panel 4: The person navigates the obstacle by jumping, fighting, swimming, or taking appropriate action.

Panel 5: The person is hurrying along a road, up a hill, or through any terrain. In the distance, a house is visible.

Panel 6: The person arrives at the house, where another person is waiting who is very happy to see him or her. They can say something to each other here.

Have students show and explain their comics to a partner, a teacher, or the class.

Activity 2: Students should produce another comic of the same length (one horizontal page, six panels), creating their own narrative using speech, symbols, and facial expressions. Have students create a script that explains what happens in each panel before they create the actual comic itself. Allow them to share these with a partner or the teacher and see if the reader can determine the action without a large amount of explanation.

I have found that these comics are generally a source of great pride for the students. Teachers can share their enthusiasm by binding the comics into a book and making copies for each student to take home. Displaying their work in the classroom or in a public area within the school often invites interest and enthusiasm from other students.

INSTRUCTION MANUAL IN SEQUENTIAL ART

Grade Level: 2–5

Goal: To understand how sequences of images can convey messages and be used for purposes other than comic book storytelling.

Lesson: Bring in a simple instruction manual that doesn't use words (IKEA instructions are ideal for this). Display it for the students and discuss with them how the sequences and codes (such as arrows) are used to explain a procedure for which we would normally use words.

Activity: Have the students create a set of instructions for a simple procedure (opening a door, taking an elevator, crossing a street, setting a table). The instructions should use no words, but should use symbols and colors. Creating a script that lays out what is contained within each panel first can be very helpful. The entire "manual "should be no fewer than six panels (a single, horizontal sheet of 8 1/2-by-11-inch paper) and no more than twelve (two horizontal sheets).

Have the students show their work and explain how their manual describes the procedure in question. Creating a book out of the manuals to keep in the classroom can be fun for students and visitors.

CREATION COLLABORATION

Grade Level: 3–12

Goal: To understand how the two elements of sequential storytelling—writing and art—come together to create the narrative and how the writer and artist must collaborate to establish this unity.

Lesson: Each form of storytelling (writing and art) creates a different vision and perspective in each storyteller. Creating a single narrative of these perspectives exemplifies the unity at the heart of sequential art.

Activity: Students should be split into groups of two, each group made of one writer and one artist. Students should be comfortable in their roles, but high-level, realistic art is not necessary. Personal style is ideal, and even stick figures can tell an effective story if used creatively.

Together, the two-student groups should discuss and create a general profile for two characters (a hero and a villain, a boyfriend and a girlfriend, a boss and an employee, a doctor and a patient, two best friends) and a general situation from which a dramatic plot can be built (a hero stops a robbery in progress, a girlfriend proposes to a boyfriend, a boss fires an employee, a doctor saves a patient's life, two best friends have an adventure in the forest). Naturally, younger students may need prompting, and it's helpful to check several times throughout the process with children up to sixth grade.

The writer takes this plot outline and writes a script of no fewer than two nine-panel pages and no more than three nine-panel pages. The script should describe each panel (in how much detail is up to the writer, with the understanding that the artist will have to draw what he describes), including character, action, and dialogue (which should be kept to a minimum).

The writer goes through the script with the artist. The two should feel free to make changes based on any useful suggestions of the artist.

The artist sketches the script in pencil, interpreting or even changing the writer's descriptions as appropriate, so long as the thrust and throughline of the story and characters are maintained. The artist should make sure to leave room for the eventual addition of word balloons. The artist goes over the pencil art with the writer. The two should feel free to make changes based on any useful suggestions of the writer. The writer should then produce word balloons with the agreed-upon dialogue and cut them out in preparation for pasting.

The artist produces the final comic. Depending on how much time is available, this can be in simple pencil sketches, inked pictures, or even inked and colored images into which the word balloons are then pasted. Allow the artists to take this assignment as homework, keeping in mind that the artist has more time- and labor-intensive work to do than the writer.

Discuss with students how they saw their various roles, focusing on the things the writer was responsible for, the things the artist was responsible for, the things that were difficult about the collaboration, and the things that collaboration made easier.

Again, sending copies home to families and collecting or displaying the works in the classroom can instill a great sense of pride.

TIME IN SEQUENTIAL ART

Grade Level: 5–8

Goal: To learn the three distinct ways in which time appears to pass in sequential art.

Lesson: The form of sequential art exists for a single purpose, which is to make time appear to pass. Motion and sound are the key elements to this illusion. There are three ways the form uses motion and sound to accomplish this: gutters, symbols, and words. (The illustrations in chapter 2 provide excellent examples; feel free to put them in a PowerPoint for the students to see.)

1. Gutter. The space between the panels is called the *gutter*. By showing you the beginning of an action in the first panel and an intermediate or final step in the second panel, the artist leaves it to your imagination to complete the action itself.

> *Example.* Panel 1 has a picture of a man squatting on one side of a gap, preparing to jump. The far side of the gap is visible at the far end of the panel. Panel 2 depicts

the man landing on the far side of the gap, while the side he started on is still visible. No jump has occurred visually, but we understand that the man has jumped.

2. Symbols. Symbols are the language of sequential art, and the form has developed special iconography, which we understand to mean certain things.

Example. A single panel has the edge of a gap at one end and another edge at the far end. Suspended between them is a man in a leaping posture. In this image, no time is passing. It may as well be a still photograph because the man appears to be suspended. Draw two speed lines from his back, down to the edge of the gap behind him. The symbol imbues the man with a sense of motion.

3. Words. In order for a word or sound to be produced and heard, time must pass.

Example. In a single panel with two people looking at one another, no time is passing. Draw a word balloon that says "Hello" from the mouth of one figure. As we understand that a word must be spoken and heard, we understand that time must be passing.

Activity 1: Two-panel story. There is a person who is happy. Something happens to him. He becomes sad. Direct students to depict this story in two panels, using the gutter, symbols, and words to create the transition of time from one panel to the next.

Activity 2: Storyboard. A passage from a book is provided. The passage should be no more than a few paragraphs and should depict a limited number of actions over the course of a short amount of time. The actions may contain, but should not be limited to, a brief conversation. Students are directed to "translate" the passage from prose into sequential art using the gutter, symbols, and words to create the transition of time from one panel to the next.

EDITING SEQUENCE

Grade Level: 7–12

Goal: To understand how malleable a narrative sequence of panels can be and the effects different choices can have on a story.

Text Used: *Houdini: The Handcuff King* by Jason Lutes and Nick Bertozzi (see chapter 6)

Lesson: Pages 62–74 in *Houdini: The Handcuff King* feature a suspenseful sequence depicting Houdini's escape from handcuffs and chains while sinking under the Charles River. Houdini's actions are intercut with reactions of the crowd above to help create tension. Can anything be done to make this sequence more suspenseful? More focused? More lyrical? Much like editing sentences changes the nature of a paragraph or story, editing panels changes the nature of the sequence. Provide copies of pages 62–74 of *Houdini: The Handcuff King* to students and direct them to alter the sequence so that the intent of the scene (Houdini escaping from a deathtrap) remains intact but is conveyed in a different way.

Activity: In addition to the above sequence, provide students with pencils, paper, and scissors. Students should cut out the panels so that they can be rearranged. Some possibilities for editing:

Remove the panels featuring the crowd of onlookers to sharpen the focus and intensity.

Remove the panels featuring Houdini escaping to heighten the perspective of the onlookers and thus their suspense.

Remove certain panels from Houdini's actions to give the sequence greater speed and flow.

Add panels (stick figures are fine—just enough to understand what should be happening in the added panels) to lengthen the sequence and give a greater sense of the specifics of action and the amount of time passing.

Add thought balloons to the Houdini sequence to heighten readers' understanding of Houdini's personality. Is he calm or panicky? Is he thinking about exactly what he has to do, or what he's going to eat for dinner later?

The edited pages will probably not conform to a standard page shape. Students can tape or glue the new sequences onto blank paper. The point here is simply to get a sense of how sequence works in the GN form. Once the students are done, let them explain what they did, why they did it, and what effect they think it had and why.

PERSPECTIVE

Grade Level: 9–12

Goal: To understand the nature of perspective in sequential art, visual media, and life in general.

Text Used: Any superhero genre GN with a fight sequence between a hero and a villain should do, but volumes from the Marvel Masterworks series or the DC Chronicles series (see chapter 6) are ideal.

Lesson: Perspective is the phenomenon by which different people view the same events in different ways. It ultimately determines which characters in a story the reader will identify with or have sympathy for. This is most common and extreme in terms of morality and ethics: what one person thinks is right, another may think is wrong. But this can be represented in visual terms through depicting an event from one person's point of view and then the other person's. An excellent example of this is found in the exaggerated actions of superheroes and supervillains. Battles between good and evil are commonplace within superhero comics, but they are nearly always seen from an objective perspective (presenting only the actions themselves) or from the superhero's point of view (depicting his thoughts during the battle or using a visual perspective that invites reader identification with the hero).

Activity 1: Select a sequence that depicts a battle between a superhero and supervillain. The sequence chosen should depict a confrontation, a physical battle, and a decisive ending within the space of three or four pages. We will use the battle between Spider-Man and the Vulture in *Marvel Masterworks Amazing Spider-Man,* volume 7, pages 108 (bottom panel) through 112 (top panel) as an example.

Step 1. Ignoring the rest of the narrative, have students rescript the battle so that only the villain's internal monologue (the words in his thought balloons) is "heard." Invent motive, explanation of recent past (why the battle began), the character's feelings as he appears to be winning and begins to lose, how the character feels about his enemy and why. If you like, you may also have students rescript any conversation that occurs (within speech balloons) to accommodate a shift in sympathy and identification between hero and villain.

Step 2. Combine the new script with the comic page, allowing the students to speak the dialogue as they go through the panel sequence, either in small groups or before the class. Discuss how it has changed the tenor of the scene and how elements such as motivation and backstory change the perspective of a story and our sympathy for and identification with a character.

Activity 2: Discuss which visual elements of the storytelling define audience sympathy and identification. Consider "camera" placement (the point from which the events are being observed), which determines which character appears in a physically superior position. Consider also facial expressions, body language, impact effects (which define who is hitting and being hit harder), and shading of backgrounds (lighter for heroes, darker for villains?). Students must, of course, suspend all previous knowledge of recognizable characters in this discussion.

Interested students should be encouraged to create a new sequence of panels shifting all these factors and combining it with their new scripts to create a sequence of actions essentially identical to the first, but with the perspective reversed.

OBJECTS OF ART

Grade Level: 11–12

Goal: To understand the GN through its art, via the personal style of the artist, its design, and as a physical object.

Texts Used: *The Arrival* by Shaun Tan (see chapter 6); *Salem Brownstone* by John Harris Dunning and Nikhil Singh (see chapter 7); and *Jimmy Corrigan: The Smartest Kid on Earth* by Chris Ware (see chapter 7)

Lesson: Although art is an essential part of any sequential narrative, the aesthetic element sometimes rises above the norm to make the GN in question a unique artistic object. Provide the three texts to each student if possible, or have at least three to five copies to pass around the class. It is not necessary to know the stories, though if you desire, students can read the GNs in question to deepen their understanding of how the art reflects the narrative and themes therein. Allow students ample time to study the books, paying special attention to (1) the distinctive style of the figural work, line work, coloring, tone, and style—the "personality" of the art; (2) the design of the pages—their composition and the size, shape, and number of panels on each; (3) the physical form of the object itself: its size, weight, shape, texture, and appearance.

Discussion/Essay Questions:

What does the style of the art make you feel and why? What tone is it trying to convey, and how does it do this? What techniques does it use?

How are the characters visually depicted, and how does this depiction make you feel about them? What does the color (or lack of color) convey? Does the depiction of the environments help you imagine how they would be experienced through any others senses?

How does the design of the book reflect on the contents? Does the size of the panels make reading them more or less comfortable? Does the size of the panels create a sense of openness or claustrophobia? Does the density or sparseness of panels on a page change the visual flow of the story?

Does the physical object itself suggest anything? Is it meant to resemble anything in particular? What visual and physical characteristics of the covers have an unusual effect? What general characteristics of the pages (as opposed to the specific art on the pages) have an unusual effect? Why might the artist intend the physical characteristics of a GN to suggest something other than a GN?

9

GRAPHIC NOVELS FOR DISCUSSION

THE LESSON PLANS IN THIS CHAPTER FUNCTION AS BOOK studies—analyses of individual GNs or groups of GNs sharing a common theme. The questions that form the body of each lesson can be used to lead discussions or build essays. As with analysis of the novel, the characters, themes, and messages are studied, but special attention is given to the way they are uniquely crafted within the sequential art form.

As in chapter 8, the entries are listed by grade level. The grade levels are predominantly 5 through 12, as most GNs with themes rich enough for in-depth analysis are written for this age group, as is the case with novels.

HISTORY SUPPLEMENTS

Grade Level: 3–12

Lesson: History curricula educate in the larger sweep and currents of history, so making historical figures and specific events come alive for students can often be tricky. GNs are ideal for their ability to engage readers in subjects they might otherwise be reluctant to pursue, and they are generally not an extremely time-consuming read. Assign a GN that can be read in a single evening, with a story focusing on the particular period in history you are currently covering to help humanize the lesson.

Following is a list of common curricular historical people, events, and issues, along with corresponding GNs to assign that will invite a worthwhile discussion.

Ancient History

Age of Bronze series (11–12)

Beowulf (11–12)

Book of Genesis (11–12)

King David (11–12)

Civil Rights

Matthew Henson: Arctic Adventurer (3–5)

Satchel Paige: Striking Out Jim Crow (5–7)

Captain America: Truth (9–10)

Incognegro (9–10)

Nat Turner (11–12)

a selection from the Cartoon History series (9–10)

Civil War

Gettysburg: The Graphic Novel (5–7)

The Murder of Abraham Lincoln (9–10)

a selection from the Cartoon History series (9–10)

Cold War

T-Minus: The Race to the Moon (6–8)

Red Menace (9–10)

Laika (9–10)

a selection from the Cartoon History series (9–10)

Current Events

A.D.: New Orleans after the Deluge (11–12)

The 9/11 Report: A Graphic Adaptation (11–12)

Great Depression

The Castaways (6–8)

The Storm in the Barn (5–7)

a selection from the Cartoon History series (9–10)

Historical Personalities

Matthew Henson: Arctic Adventurer (3–5)

Amelia Earhart: This Broad Ocean (5–7)

Gettysburg: The Graphic Novel (5–7)

Houdini: The Handcuff King (6–8)

Satchel Paige: Striking Out Jim Crow (5–7)

The Murder of Abraham Lincoln (9–10)

Nat Turner (11–12)

King David (11–12)

Action Philosophers (11–12)

Immigration/Assimilation

The Arrival (6–8)

James Sturm's America: God, Gold, and Golems (11–12)

A Contract with God and Other Tenement Stories (11–12)

Middle East

Persepolis (11–12)

Pride of Baghdad (9–10)

Waltz with Bashir: A Lebanon War Story (11–12)

World War II

City of Spies (4–6)

Captain America: Truth (9–10)

EC Archives: Two-Fisted Tales series (9–10)

Parade (with Fireworks) (9–10)

The Complete Maus: A Survivor's Tale (9–10)

X-Men: Magneto Testament (11–12)

a selection from the Cartoon History series (9–10)

Discussion/Essay Questions

Did the GN reflect what you had learned about the particular person or event studied? Do you think it was an accurate depiction of the time and events?

Did the historical figures in the story act as you expected, based on what you knew about them? What surprised you?

Did the GN omit anything or add anything? Was a person or detail omitted or included that made it differ from the historical events as studied? Why do you think the author made that choice and what did it accomplish?

THE STORM IN THE BARN

Grade Level: 5–7

Text Used: *The Storm in the Barn* by Matt Phelan (see chapter 6)

Lesson: *The Storm in the Barn* is a classic coming-of-age story with elements of fairy tales and folktales that help produce a tone that is at once magical and, through the washed-out and powerful art, incredibly evocative of a real place and time. These archetypal narrative elements, as well as the way stories and storytelling are treated within the tale, make *The Storm in the Barn* an extraordinary homage to stories themselves.

Discussion/Essay Questions

How does the artist use color? Is it plentiful or spare? What is it intended to make you feel? Why does it work that way?

What events throughout the story help Jack grow up? In what ways do they do that?

What elements from fairy tales and folktales appear in the story? What similarities does *The Storm in the Barn* itself have to fairy tales and folktales?

What does the weather in all its various forms (storm, drought, dust devil) represent in the story?

Stories and narratives are used in various ways through the book (even within the dedication). What role do stories play within *The Storm in the Barn*? What kinds of stories are they? How are they used? How do they make characters feel?

THE ARRIVAL

Grade Level: 6–8

Text Used: *The Arrival* by Shaun Tan (see chapter 6)

Lesson: Using an extremely complex and subtle style, employing the techniques of both sequential art and storybook art, *The Arrival* tells the archetypal story of a man who travels to a strange land. Using wordless narrative to exemplify its protagonist's isolation and visual metaphor to lend an archetypal power to the journeys of various immigrants in the story, the book strikes a deeply emotional tone. At the same time, the experiences are related through a physical object that—through color palette, texture, and page composition—resembles an ancient family photo album more than a GN, to suggest that we are looking back through the years at an actual life.

Discussion/Essay Questions

Why are no actual words used in *The Arrival*? What effect does this have on the reader?

Is *The Arrival* a colorful book? In what ways, when, and why does the color change? What effect does the use of color have on the overall reading experience?

The city the immigrant arrives in isn't real, but what sort of a city is it? Is it meant to suggest any real city, either contemporary or historical? Which one and in what ways does it suggest that place and time?

How is visual metaphor used? Are the immigrants who tell their stories of departure and escape really running from giants with vacuum cleaners or tentacles, or through vast mazes? What are these things meant to represent? Why do you think the main character left his own homeland?

What is the GN as a physical object meant to resemble? In what ways? What effect does it mean to achieve by doing this?

GENDER PORTRAYALS IN GRAPHIC NOVELS

Grade Level: 6–9

Texts Used: *Amelia Earhart: This Broad Ocean* by Sarah Stewart Taylor and Ben Towle (see chapter 6), *Smile* by Raina Telgemeier (see chapter 6), *The Plain Janes* by Cecil Castellucci and Jim Rugg (see chapter 7). Optionally, *Re-Gifters* by Mike Carey, Marc Hempel, and Sonny Liew (see chapter 7), or *Rapunzel's Revenge* by Shannon Hale, Dean Hale, and

Nathan Hale (see chapter 6) can be used to either replace one of the above or to further support the lesson.

Lesson: While the male protagonist's journey is usually a literal one—from one geographic location to another, facing physical challenges that impart wisdom along the way—the female protagonist's journey is often a figurative one. If her "adventure" requires her to leave her community, it is generally and immediately into the heart of a new one. The female protagonist's challenges are socially oriented, overcoming community pressures and social expectations. The female protagonist's "enemy" tends to be the position that her family, friends, and community have set up for her and expect her to occupy.

Amelia Earhart: This Broad Ocean features the struggle of young Grace, inspired by a meeting with the famous aviatrix, to make her way into the larger world. In *The Plain Janes*, Jane must overcome her new community's inflexible standards as she overcomes her own fears. *Smile*'s Raina must face her own physical changes and the altered perceptions they engender in her friends and family.

Discussion/Essay Questions

Do the female protagonists in these stories go on great journeys, or are their "adventures" more a matter of "going somewhere" within themselves and changing the view of their friends, families, schools, or towns?

What changes occur within the lives of each of the three protagonists personally?

What changes do each of these characters bring about within their communities?

Why do you think female protagonists most often struggle against social forces and perceptions rather than physical obstacles or actual enemies? Is there a historical reason or basis for this? Can you think of events in history where women have been required to do this?

AMERICAN BORN CHINESE

Grade Level: 9–12

Text Used: *American Born Chinese* by Gene Luen Yang (see chapter 7)

Lesson: *American Born Chinese* tells three apparently disconnected tales: the Monkey King of Chinese mythology strives to gain the respect of the other gods; Jin Wang, a Chinese American student, wants to fit in but must deal with the racism of peers as well as the feelings he harbors in his own heart; Danny must endure a visit from his cousin Chin-Kee, a conglomeration of foul Chinese stereotypes. The stories, in the end, turn out to be intertwined in a shocking way that masterfully highlights the themes of judgment, friendship, and self-esteem.

Central to the entire book is the use of a deep irony, a reversal of expectations that moves through not only the narrative, but the very craft of the book itself, as it employs a slyly simple, classic comic book style of page layouts, draftsmanship, codes, and color palette to tell an exceedingly complex narrative filled with difficult themes central to human social interaction.

Discussion/Essay Questions

What does Jin Wang want in life? What does the Monkey King want? What does Danny want? Is there any similarity in their motives and desires?

What does Chin-Kee represent? How does it relate to Jin Wang's emotional situation?

Why does Danny's story appear to take place within a television sitcom? What does it change about the way we view his story? Does it make certain things easier to accept? How does this relate to the three overall stories?

Does the book use generally standard sequential art page layout, character design, speech and sound effects, and color palette? Why does it present itself in a visually simple style given that technique and technology are capable of a great deal more visual sophistication?

In what ways does the narrative play with standard structure? Are the stories told chronologically? Do they fit together in a standard way? How does this highlight the overall themes and message?

CIVIL WAR (MARVEL COMICS)

Grade Level: 9–12

Text Used: *Civil War* by Mark Millar and Steve McNiven (see chapter 7)

Lesson: A superhero-related disaster leads to a government sanction, requiring all costumed crime fighters to reveal their identities and work for law enforcement agencies or go to jail. This fractures the superhero community, with one side led by Captain America, who believes that submitting would put too much power in the hands of too few people, and the other led by Iron Man, who believes that the immediate safety of the community comes first and that the heroes must capitulate. The ensuing war of beliefs (and fists) morally compromises several heroes and, as is appropriate for a tale centering on an issue as complex as privacy versus security, ends ambiguously.

Discussion/Essay Questions

Why was this GN called *Civil War*? What is a civil war, and how do the actions that occur in the story reflect that?

Where do you stand on the issue? What dangers do you see as a result of superheroes either revealing their identities and working for the government or continuing to function independently? What issues in real-world politics could this situation be compared to?

Were you expecting Captain America, the symbol of our country, to go against the government? Why? Why did he do it? Were you expecting Iron Man, the millionaire industrialist, to eschew independence and cooperate with the government? Why? Why did he do it?

What do you think about Spider-Man's dilemma? Was he being unfairly manipulated? Why and by whom? Why do you think he switched sides? Do you think he was right to do it? What personal consequences did the events of the story have for him and other heroes (Mr. Fantastic/Reed Richards, for example)? How do these consequences affect their actions?

Did these heroes comport themselves heroically, act in a responsible way? Even if you grant that there was no way to avoid a fight, what actions do you think either side took that pushed the limits of good conscience? Did one side act irresponsibly first?

Which one and how? Is it possible to act responsibly and with good conscience in a war? Should there be rules for war? If so, how can we expect combatants to adhere to them?

Was the issue resolved in the end, or was the heart of the issue left unsettled for other reasons? Should it have ended differently? How?

HEROES THEN AND NOW

Grade Level: 9–12

Texts Used: Either *The Odyssey* by Homer, adapted by Tim Mucci and illustrated by Ben Caldwell (see chapter 6), which is a faster read and more stylistically comparable to the superhero texts, or *The Odyssey* adapted by Gareth Hinds (see chapter 7), which is a more involved and realistic interpretation; either *Ultimate Spider-Man, Volume 1: Power and Responsibility* by Brian Michael Bendis and Mark Bagley (see chapter 7) or *Superman for All Seasons* by Jeph Loeb and Tim Sale (see chapter 7)

Lesson: Homer's epic poem codified many of the heroic traits and established the foundations of heroic adventure that we see today in adventure books, superhero comics, and action movies. But for all that modern heroes owe the poem, a comparison with modern heroic adventure reveals a significant evolution (or devolution) of the heroic character over the years. While the older and wiser Odysseus tends to use intelligence over brawn, and his quest is merely to return to his family and set his house in order, his ultimate virtue appears to be his fealty to the gods, whom he relies upon in many ways. The younger, more muscle-centric Spider-Man and Superman reflect a more modern (and American) philosophy of individual achievement and self-reliance.

Discussion/Essay Questions

At what age or at what point in life is Odysseus as compared to Spider-Man or Superman? Do you have the sense that they are just starting out in life, or that they have many adventures behind them?

What is Odysseus's quest? What is he trying to do and why? Who is he responsible to, and does he live up to this responsibility in every case? Why do Spider-Man and Superman fight crime? How did they learn their sense of responsibility to their communities? Are they always successful in living up to this responsibility?

What are the challenges Odysseus faces? Are they all physical in nature? What abilities, skills, and powers are required to overcome them? What challenges do Spider-Man and Superman need to overcome? What is required of them to win? Is Odysseus's intelligence or his physical skill and power more important to his success? Which is more important to the success of Spider-Man and Superman? What do the challenges a hero must overcome say about that hero?

What role do religion and faith play in Odysseus's quest? Are the gods his allies or enemies (or both)? What is the nature of his relationship with them? Do religion and faith play any part in the adventures of Spider-Man and Superman? What, if anything, seems to take its place in their adventures? Does Odysseus's ultimate servitude to the gods make him less heroic? Does Spider-Man's and Superman's mastery of their own destinies make them more or less heroic? Why do you think religion and faith are mainly absent from modern heroic adventure?

KINGDOM COME

Grade Level: 9–12

Text Used: *Kingdom Come* by Mark Waid and Alex Ross (see chapter 7)

Lesson: *Kingdom Come* is an examination of politics, government, morality, responsibility, war, and consequences on a superheroic scale. It follows a retired Superman as he must make a stand against a generation of violent young crime fighters and help society determine just who it wants to believe in. Powerfully served by the photorealistic painted art of Alex Ross, the story has a weight and sense of reality that supports its consideration of significant real-world issues.

Discussion/Essay Questions

What are the differences between the older generation of superheroes, like Superman, and the newer generation of superheroes, like Magog? How do they act differently? How do they treat criminals differently? How do they treat "normal" people differently? Can you make a case for both sides?

The Specter speaks of "Superman's greatest and most necessary failing . . . his inability to see himself as the inspiration he is." Why is this a "necessary" failure on Superman's part? How has he served as an inspiration? What have people and other superheroes lost without this inspiration? Do you feel that people in Superman's position should have a right to have a life of their own and retire, or are they always in some way obligated to the people who look up to them?

What are the differences between Superman's philosophy and Wonder Woman's? How would "normal" people fare in a world overseen by either one of them, considering their ideas about protecting citizenry and punishing criminals? Can you make a case to support either philosophy?

In what ways does religion play a part in the story? Does God Himself seem to be involved, or is faith the crucial aspect? What is the practical difference in people's lives between God and faith in God? Does religion or faith seem to be a positive or negative force, or both, in the story? In what ways?

How is the art different than art you might see in other comics and GNs? What effect does the style of art have on the story, the themes, and the ideas presented within?

SHAKESPEARE COMPARISON

Grade Level: 9–12

Texts Used: Shakespeare is the most popularly adapted author in the GN format, and there is no shortage of either plays or styles to choose from (see chapter 7). This lesson can be done with various levels of depth and complexity. At minimum, one original play should be read in whole or part (again, depending on the complexity chosen) and one GN adaptation of that play. At maximum, choose one original play and two adaptations of that play. In the latter case, I highly recommend that one of the adaptations be from the Classical Comics line (see chapter 7), in either the quick text or plain text versions. As an alternative, you can use *Kill Shakespeare* by McCreery, Del Col, and Belanger (see chapter 7) to illustrate qualities in the original works not through direct adaptation, but through a world adapted from and peopled with Shakespeare's plays and characters.

Lesson: Varying levels of depth and complexity are possible with this lesson, appropriate to age group and amount of time to be spent. In the simplest form, a single scene from one of Shakespeare's plays should be chosen and read aloud in class (see the following activities). The same scene from the GN adaptation would then be read or, ideally, displayed for the entire class to see as it is read.

A more complex lesson would entail assigning one of Shakespeare's plays for homework, holding discussions as it is read in accordance with classroom curriculum. As each act is completed, assign the same act from the GN adaptation. Alternatively, at the completion of the entire play, assign the GN adaptation of that play.

Another possibility would be, upon the completion of the assigned play and pertinent discussions, to assign two GN adaptations of the same play. Again, I highly recommend that one of them be the Classical Comics quick text or plain text version. An excellent way to set up a comparison is to choose one of the adaptations that changes the setting of the original play. The manga Shakespeare series has many such interpretations.

Finally, a horse of a rather different color is *Kill Shakespeare,* which doesn't adapt the Bard's plays, but imagines a world drawn from several of them. The characters' motives and behavior are well adapted from Shakespeare's originals, and many of the play's original tones and themes are presented in fresh circumstances and from new perspectives. After lessons involving *Hamlet, Othello,* or one of *Henry IV Part I, Henry IV Part II,* or *The Merry Wives of Windsor,* allow students to select the character of Hamlet, Iago, or Falstaff and to read *Kill Shakespeare* with a particular focus on the chosen character.

Activity (optional): Rather than simply reading a scene from one of the plays out loud in class, have student volunteers perform the scene in question. This does require more planning and time, but the visual element creates a level of comparison to the visual nature of the GN adaptation that simply reading aloud does not.

Discussion/Essay Questions

For a single scene comparison

> Does the scene seem shorter or longer in the adaptation? How is that accomplished? Is anything omitted? If so, why?

> Which character seems most powerful or important in the original scene reading (or performance)? Does it have to do with the dialogue as written, as read, or as performed?

> Which character seems most powerful or important in the adapted scene? What aspects make the character seem that way? Does it have to do with the positioning of the characters, either their placement in the panel or the poses of their bodies? Does it have to do with the way their expressions were illustrated or the way they were costumed or colored?

> Did reading the adaptation make you see or understand the scene in a different way?

For reading the original play and one adaptation

> What, if anything, was omitted from the adaptation? If so, why do you think the adaptors chose to omit it? Does the visual aspect of the adaptation make up for omissions of dialogue? Can an adaptation serve the original work better in some ways by abridging it?

Do the characters look and behave in the adaptation as you thought they would, based on the play itself? What, if anything, changes about them, and how is this change presented (in size, coloring, costuming, facial features, expression, body language)?

What scenes in the adaptation are interpreted the most dramatically? Are those the most dramatic scenes in the play itself? If not, why do you think the adaptor chose to give them more weight? What techniques does the adaptor use to convey the heightened drama of that scene (space, action, color, effects)?

If the setting of the adaptation is not the same setting as the original play, why do you think the setting has been changed? Does it serve to highlight a theme of the play or reflect the actions or feelings of the characters? Does it make the play more engaging to read?

Are the themes and messages Shakespeare was trying to put across still clear in the adaptation? What does the adaptation do to support them, highlight them, or bring them out?

For two adaptations

Are the characters recognizable from one adaptation to the next? Do they look similar (features, costuming, coloring)? Do they act similarly (expressions, body language)? Do the adaptors seem to favor one particular character in a way the other adaptors do not?

Does one adaptation interpret particular scenes more dramatically than the other? Did one make the play more engaging, dramatic, or understandable than the other? If so, how?

Do the adaptations use different costuming, eras or settings? Does one work better than the other? If so, why?

Does one adaptation omit material that the other did not? Do both adaptations convey the overall story effectively? If not, how does the adaptation in question fail? What did it not do that the successful adaptation does?

Are there themes and messages that one adaptation focuses on that the other does not? Is this intentional? In what ways does one adaptation bring these themes out more effectively?

Do you think Shakespeare meant for there to be one "correct" interpretation of his play?

For Kill Shakespeare

What are three things the character in question (Hamlet, Iago, Falstaff) does that reflect that character's personality in the original? Does the character seem like the same person in both? What do the character's actions tell you about him? Has the character grown at all between the original story and *Kill Shakespeare*? From what point in the play (or after the play) does the character seem drawn?

What themes from the original plays are carried through into *Kill Shakespeare*? What scenes or moments highlight these themes? What themes and ideas occur within the graphic novel that you have not seen suggested in the original play? Do they seem out of place, or do they fit within the framework of Shakespeare's world?

SUPERMAN'S CULTURAL EVOLUTION

Grade Level: 9–12

Texts Used: *The Superman Chronicles, Volume 1* by Siegel and Shuster (see the DC Chronicles series, chapter 6); *Superman for All Seasons* by Loeb and Sale (see chapter 7); *Superman: Birthright* by Waid and Yu (see chapter 7)

Lesson: The character of Superman has developed and been adapted over time in a way that exemplifies the social trends and perspectives of the different eras in which he's interpreted. His earliest adventures (in *The Superman Chronicles*) are surprisingly hard-edged and morally uncompromising in their judgment of corruption among the powerful. *A Superman for All Seasons* depicts a gentler character situated in an American mythology of rural idealism and sophisticated shining metropolises. *Superman: Birthright* is a darker story of holding onto your heritage even as it is manipulated against you, and is a tale that seems to resonate for a more ambiguous age.

Discussion/Essay Questions

What aspects of Superman's character are similar and different through the different depictions? What are his powers? How is he likely to deal with his enemies? How is the interaction between Lois Lane and Superman/Clark Kent depicted?

What world does Superman inhabit in each depiction? Does he seem "born" of an urban or rural environment? What things are associated with each of these types of places? What was happening in the world when Superman was first created? Which depiction seems darker; which world seems the most dangerous to inhabit?

How does each depiction delve into Superman's psychology? What do we know and understand about him? What seem to be the parameters of his mission and what events and people in the course of his life have caused him to take on that mission? What do we know about his origins? What role does Clark Kent play? In which depiction is he the real person and in which is he the disguise?

How does the art differ from depiction to depiction? In what ways does it become more sophisticated? How is action conveyed? How long is each of the stories? Is action a greater or lesser part of the stories as they become more sophisticated? What is the point or moral of each story?

Who does Superman fight against, and what do they represent? What social events and currents of the time seemed to be undesirable/dangerous based on each depiction? How do the writer and artist of each story seem to feel about these issues? Does popular entertainment intend to comment on the world around it, or is it simply incidental? *Should* popular entertainment comment on the world around it?

WATCHMEN

Grade Level: 11–12

Text Used: *Watchmen* by Alan Moore and Dave Gibbons (see chapter 7)

Lesson: Moore's *Watchmen* may be the most pivotal GN in history. With its political agenda, its deep character studies, and deconstruction of the form itself, it has an array of issues and themes ripe for close study. I would not recommend trying to encompass the entire work in a single study, however, and I have highlighted three areas below that would make a strong focus for class discussions or as a written report.

History/politics. Watchmen was originally released in 1986, which was an intense time in U.S. political history, with the cold war moving toward a nuclear peak and Ronald Reagan's government dividing the country into a majority of conservative supporters and a minority of liberals who believed that the former actor had pulled the wool over the country's collective eyes. Many were also concerned with behind-the-scenes corruption (most notably the president's involvement in the Iran-Contra affair) and with the country one button push away from nuclear Armageddon (or so it seemed), there was a level of fear building through society that has not been felt since.

Examine what the alternate 1986 of *Watchmen* seems to be saying about the political environment of the actual 1986, with a focus on government control and the nuclear arms race with the Soviet Union, and the parallels *Watchmen* is attempting to draw between the real world and the invented world. What is Alan Moore getting at? How does he feel about politics of the day and even our potential saviors?

Superheroes. If superheroes like Superman and Batman have traditionally been upstanding moral community builders, *Watchmen*'s interpretation pulls the rug from beneath the very concept of the superhero by analyzing what a real person would have to be like to engage in such activities and the effects it would have on his or her psyche. What is Alan Moore saying about the notion of the superhero and the form of the comic book itself? What does he seem to think about those who are our apparent saviors, the very watchmen of society?

Art. Gibbons and Moore created an unprecedented melding of art and story in *Watchmen,* bringing the form's essential unity to a new level to highlight themes and narrative elements. Each chapter title page (originally the covers of the monthly *Watchmen* comics) is, in fact, the first panel of the chapter, and each one is adorned with a doomsday clock that ticks the moments down to the end of the story. The color palette creates very thick atmosphere that defines the tone of the story in a way the writing itself could never do alone. Every chapter is followed by an illustrated text piece meant to define the alternate history that is the background of the overall story. Chapter 5 ("Fearful Symmetry") all by itself is a daring experiment with the form as the first fourteen pages are an exact mirror reflection of the last fourteen pages in composition and coloring (an artistic symmetry to go with the title).

The creators of *Watchmen* have made an extraordinary effort to take advantage of the form's two constituent elements and have them support each other throughout the narrative. What effects does the art have on the story overall? How does the art highlight elements and themes of the story, differentiate the contemporary narrative from flashback, create tone, and experiment with the format itself?

AFTERWORD

As late as September 2009, we decided to bite the bullet and create a GN section in our school library. LREI—Little Red School House and Elisabeth Irwin High School—is a pre-K through twelfth grade independent school in New York City. It occupies two separate buildings and thus has two libraries. The high school library already had a solid GN section all its own. The section thrived because teen interest in the form is high. But for the lower and middle school library we had long kept the GNs locked up in 741.5. They grew there without the librarians having to make any extra effort to showcase them, and they weren't *so* easy to find that the kids eschewed everything else for them.

But the time came, the demand was high—questions were coming nearly every library period from kids new to the format wondering where the heck ours were—so as the new school year approached, I set aside a day for the transfer. Adhering to the needs and population of the school body, I set it up in several sections:

early fiction GNs (by author's last name) for prekindergarten through fourth grade

fiction GNs for fourth through eighth grades (also by author's last name and with a young adult sticker on the spine for more mature reads)

fairy tales and mythology GNs (by title)

nonfiction (by Dewey and author's last name, with all the biographies up at the front)

superheroes (by title character's name)

There are variations on how to do it, of course, but this was the best for us: we could put the GNs for older and younger readers on separate shelves, and the kids had an easy time finding exactly what they wanted, not only by general subject, but in the case of fairy tales, mythology, and superheroes, even by the specific character they wanted.

We expected that there would be a boom in GN circulation and then it would calm down and find its steady constant.

Well, as of the writing of this book, it hasn't calmed down, and it shows no signs of doing so any time soon. In fact, as word spread from student to student, the demand increased. We literally cannot keep the GNs on the shelves, nor supply new ones fast enough, and I'm not just talking about the superheroes, either. Teachers took notice; they couldn't help it if they tried. I started fielding questions about appropriate reading levels and watched as the GNs began to creep into some of the classrooms themselves. Parents became curious. Many loved that their kids were leaping into reading as they never had before; others were challenging and suspicious of the GNs (and of me for putting them there). My very, very patient fellow librarians and I answered their questions, too. Perhaps they gained a measure of relief when their children didn't start holding up liquor stores or forgetting to read "traditional" books. Regardless, the GNs are there to stay now. I couldn't remove them from the library if I wanted to.

Whether we embrace it or challenge it, we're all living in a GN world now. The kids were ahead of us. They felt the strength of the format and the way it empowered their imaginations and thus their investment in and enthusiasm for reading.

I have made this book as complete a work as possible, covered all the pertinent areas as deeply as I could. It is as definitive a work as I could make it. But it is only so for now. As with any vehicle of the imagination, the GN medium will evolve, even as education will, and the two will find a new relationship. By then, you will hopefully have gotten a good start on how to make the form work for you, how to use GNs to enrich the lives of you and your students, how to use these unique works of imagination to help make a finer world.

That's all I ask of you.

FURTHER READING

The list of reference materials is meant to supplement your library collection with a small array of reference books. This will not only round out curious students' knowledge of the form, but also provide something you can offer to skeptical teachers, administrators, or parents to help them understand exactly how much potential the form has and the complex history behind it. The titles include both history books and books on the art of the form.

The books on the second list are intended to help expand your own reservoir of knowledge on the history and craft of the sequential art form. I've endeavored to include books that are not only informative, but also extremely enjoyable.

Reference Materials

ABDO and Daughters. Comic Book Creators series. Edina, MN: ABDO and Daughters, 2006.

Eisner, Will. *Comics and Sequential Art.* New York: W. W. Norton, 2008.

Gray, Peter C. How to Draw Manga series. London: Franklin Watts Ltd., 2005–2006.

Krensky, Stephen. *Comic Book Century: The History of American Comic Books.* Breckenridge, CO: Twenty-first Century Books, 2007.

Lee, Stan. *How to Draw Comics the Marvel Way.* New York: Fireside, 1984.

O'Neil, Dennis. *DC Comics Guide to Writing Comics.* New York: Watson-Guptill, 2001.

Williams, Freddie E. II. *DC Comics Guide to Digitally Drawing Comics.* New York: Watson-Guptill, 2009.

Further Reading

Brenner, Robin. *Understanding Manga and Anime.* Westport, CT: Libraries Unlimited, 2007.

Carlin, John, Paul Karasik, and Brian Walker, eds. *Masters of American Comics.* New Haven, CT: Yale University Press, 2005.

DeHaven, Tom. *Our Hero: Superman on Earth.* New Haven, CT: Yale University Press, 2010.

Fingeroth, Danny. *Disguised as Clark Kent: Jews, Comics, and the Creation of the Super-hero*. New York: Continuum, 2008.

Fingeroth, Danny. *Superman on the Couch: What Superheroes Really Tell Us about Our-selves and Our Society*. New York: Continuum, 2004.

Hajdu, David. *The Ten-Cent Plague: The Great Comic Book Scare and How It Changed America*. New York: Picador, 2009.

Jones, Gerard. *Men of Tomorrow: Geeks, Gangsters, and the Birth of the Comic Book*. New York: Basic Books, 2005.

Lee, Stan, and George Mair. *Excelsior! The Amazing Life of Stan Lee*. New York: Fireside, 2002.

Morrison, Grant. *Supergods: What Masked Vigilantes, Miraculous Mutants, and a Sun God from Smallville Can Teach Us about Being Human*. New York: Spiegel & Grau, 2011.

Wright, Bradford W. *Comic Book Nation: The Transformation of Youth Culture in Amer-ica*. Baltimore: Johns Hopkins University Press, 2003.

REFERENCES

Bogumil, Jeff. Graphic Novel Archive, http://graphicnovelarchive.com.

Gootman, Elissa. "Superman Finds New Fans Among Reading Instructors." *New York Times,* December 26, 2007, B1, B7.

Gorg, Mallia. "Learning from the Sequence: The Use of Comics in Instruction." *ImageTexT: Interdisciplinary Comics Studies* 3, no. 3 (2007). www.english.ufl.edu/imagetext/archives/v3_3/mallia/index.shtml.

Karp, Jesse. 2008. " Eye of the Sturm: Booklist Interview with James Sturm." *Booklist* (March 15, 2008). www.booklistonline.com/default.aspx?page=show_product&pid =2428627.

Lee, Stan, and Steve Ditko. "Spider-Man!" *Amazing Fantasy 15* (August 1962): 11.

Lee, Stan, and George Mair. *Excelsior! The Amazing Life of Stan Lee*. New York: Fireside, 2002.

Little, Drego. "In a Single Bound: A Short Primer on Comics for Educators." 2005. http://education.jhu.edu/newhorizons/strategies/topics/literacy/articles/inasinglebound ashortprimeroncomicsforedu/.

Lyga, Allyson A. W., and Barry Lyga. *Graphic Novels in Your Media Center: A Definitive Guide*. Westport, CT: Libraries Unlimited, 2004.

Mann, Ron. *Comic Book Confidential* (film). Canada: Sphinx Productions, 1988.

McCloud, Scott. *Understanding Comics*. New York: Harper, 1994.

Pink, Daniel H. "Japan, Ink: Inside the Manga Industrial Complex." *Wired* 15, no. 11 (October 2007): 216–222, 261.

Siegel, Jerry, and Joe Shuster. "Revolution in San Monte, Part 2." *Action Comics* 2 (July 1938): 2.

Smetana, Linda, et al. "Using Graphic Novels in the High School Classroom: Engaging Deaf Students with a New Genre." *Journal of Adolescent and Adult Literacy* 53, no. 3 (November 2009): 228–240.

Thompson, Jason. "How Manga Conquered the U.S.: A Graphic Guide to Japan's Coolest Export." *Wired* 15, no. 11 (October 2007): 223–233.

DISCUSSION TOPIC INDEX

AUTHOR-TITLE INDEX

Page numbers in bold indicate annotations.

SUBJECT INDEX

You may also be interested in

THE READERS' ADVISORY GUIDE TO GRAPHIC NOVELS
FRANCISCA GOLDSMITH

"The American Library Association (ALA) adds another excellent and, in this case, much-needed volume to its readers' advisory library with this succinct guide ... a valuable and quite readable resource that belongs in every library's professional collection." –*VOYA*

ISBN: 978-0-8389-1008-5
136 PAGES / 6" x 9"

COTEACHING READING COMPREHENSION STRATEGIES IN SECONDARY SCHOOL LIBRARIES
JUDI MOREILLON
ISBN: 978-0-8389-1088-7

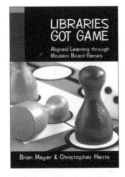

LIBRARIES GOT GAME
BRIAN MAYER AND CHRISTOPHER HARRIS
ISBN: 978-0-8389-1009-2

THE WHOLE SCHOOL LIBRARY HANDBOOK 2
EDITED BY BLANCHE WOOLLS AND DAVID V. LOERTSCHER
ISBN: 978-0-8389-1127-3

BEING INDISPENSABLE
RUTH TOOR AND HILDA K. WEISBURG
ISBN: 978-0-8389-1065-8

VIDEO GAME COLLECTION DEVELOPMENT AND MANAGEMENT
JP PORCARO AND JUSTIN HOENKE
ISBN: 978-0-8389-1146-4

OUTSTANDING BOOKS FOR THE COLLEGE BOUND
EDITED BY ANGELA CARSTENSEN FOR YALSA
ISBN: 978-0-8389-8570-0